Guy Bourdin

Guy Bourdin

Introduction by Giles de Bure

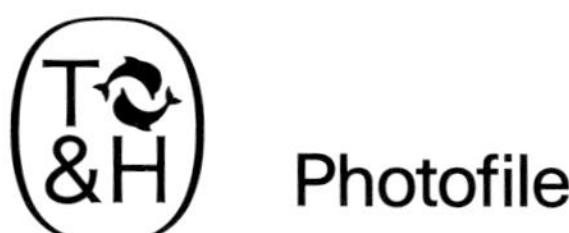

Photofile

Extending the gaze

A route along the Left Bank: Rue Férou, Rue de l'Abbaye, Place du Palais Bourbon. Meetings: Man Ray, Rue Férou, his several visits earning Bourdin something of a post-surrealist reputation; Robert Delpire, Rue de l'Abbaye, who grasps the breadth and depth of Bourdin's character at first glance and speeds him post-haste to the next stage; Edmonde Charles-Roux, Place du Palais Bourbon, editor-in-chief of *Vogue Paris*, who gives him his first commissioned subject, 'Chapeaux-Choc' ('Shocking Hats').

In 1955, it was not just the hats that were shocking. The height of elegance, the peak of chic, with a background of calves' heads and skinned rabbits. The black and white of the images softens the violence of the shock. Bourdin had yet to discover and master colour.

In Bourdin's very first images, just as in the Polaroids he took in great numbers, there is also a lightness, a freshness that brings him closer to poetic realism in the French style than to surrealism. A link to the work of Brassaï, Izis or Ronis, but with all anecdotal elements removed. Images that are generally static, and whose static nature recalls the early days of photography, when very long exposure times made buildings a favourite subject for photographers. The still, grey, mysterious and mystical Paris of Atget; the Flatiron Building in New York as photographed by Alfred Stieglitz (1903) and Edward Steichen (1904), one by day, the other by night.

Framing, composition, geometry, symmetry, contrast, texture, lines, rhythms, volumes: is it a photograph or a pure sculptural composition? Does everything converge towards a vanishing point, dematerializing and becoming unreal? It is almost a way of stripping down the image to the point of removing its effect on the senses, but not its sense. Already all the elements are there, not of Bourdin's style but of Bourdin's art.

At *Vogue* in 1955, everything was going well for him. He even acquired an unusual independence. Whatever the subject matter, he would deliver only one photograph, one that he had thought about, selected and printed himself at the exact size required for

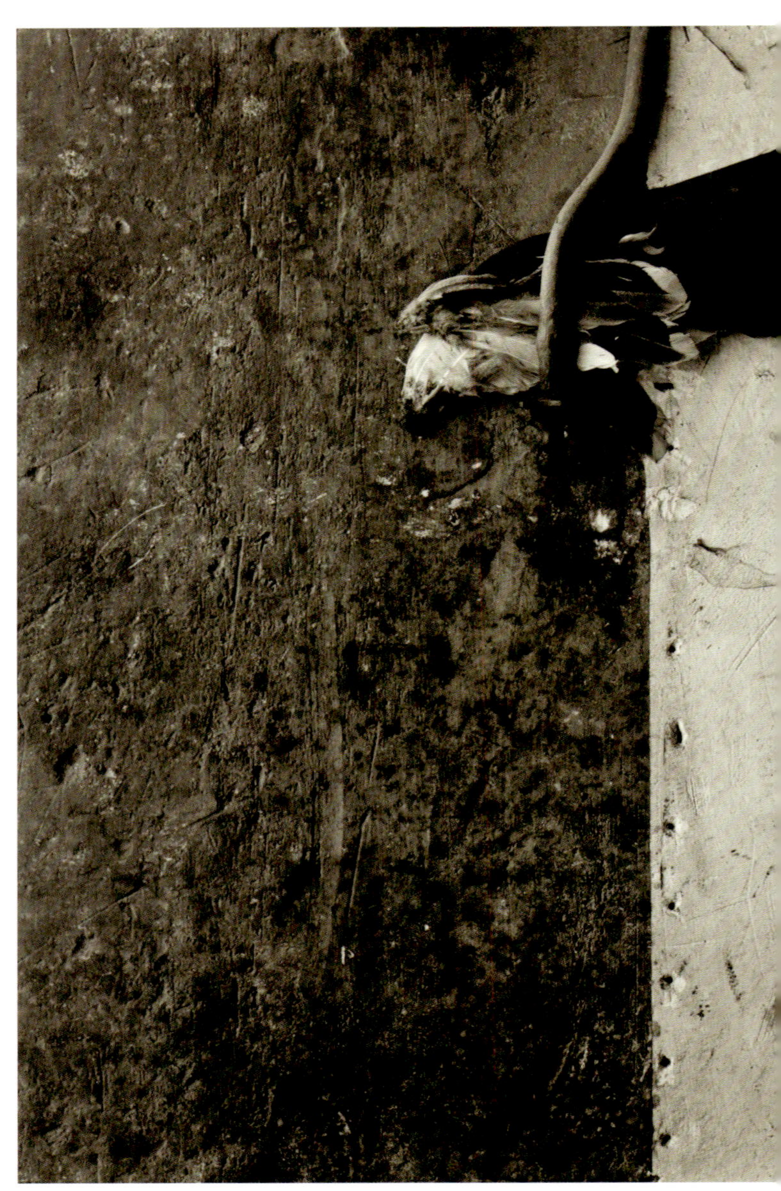

1. Guy Bourdin Archives, c. 1950–55.

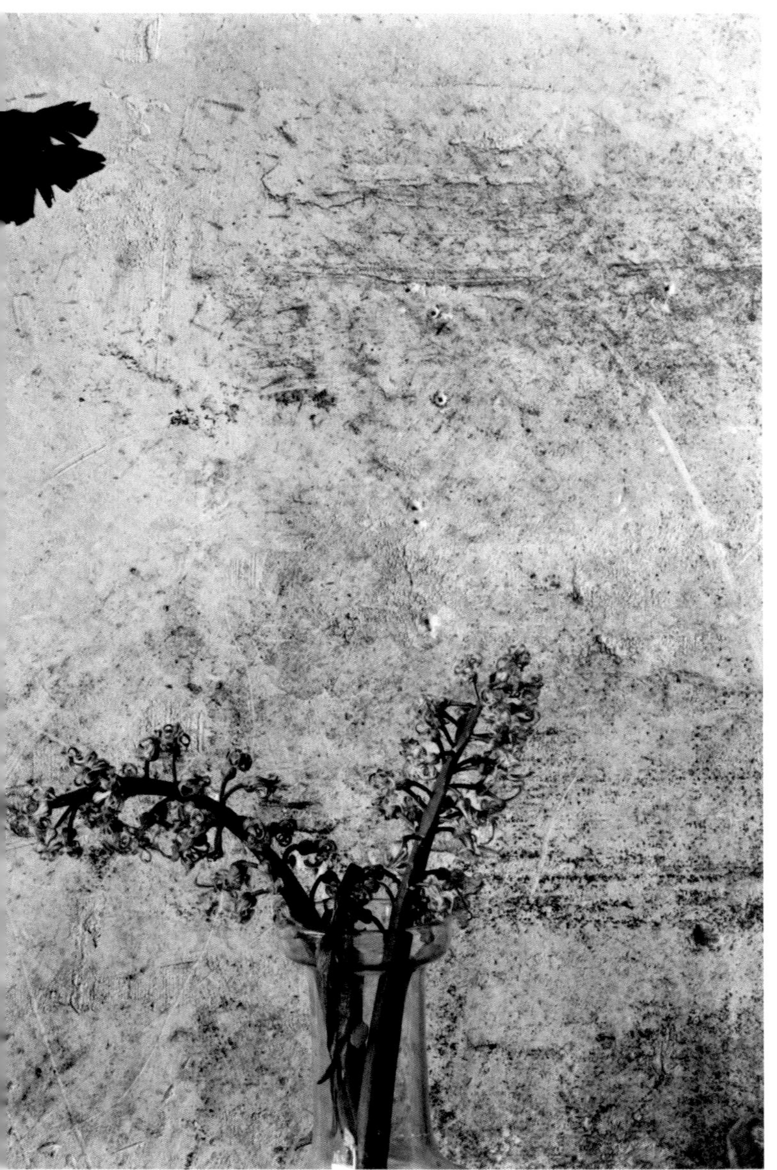

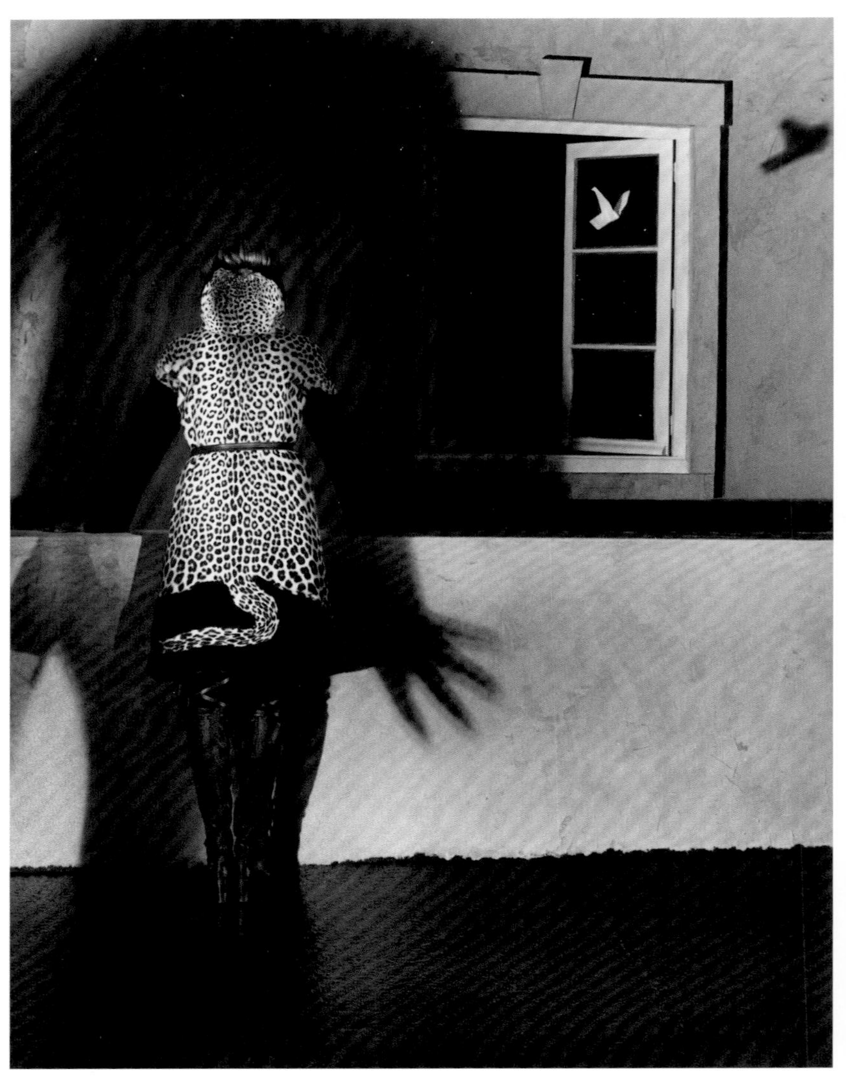

2. *Vogue France*, September 1969.

a double-page magazine spread. 'Bourdin's radicality has often been chalked up to a capricious or disdainful attitude towards the genre of fashion photography. Yet in fact his position developed out of his great conceptual and formal engagement with the magazine as his sole artistic medium. In his strict conception of his art practice, Bourdin treated the double-page spread of a magazine as a structural characteristic of his work,' wrote Alison M. Gingeras (in *Guy Bourdin*, 2006). Later, this way of taking a magazine and shaping it to fit a cause would be found in the work of other artists, such as Philippe Thomas (*Les ready-made appartiennent à tout le monde*) and Gilles Mahé (*Gratuit*).

At *Vogue*, Bourdin was a colleague of William Klein and Helmut Newton. He would never be compared to Klein, who was already definitely perceived as a 'reporter'. He was, however, often compared to Helmut Newton and still is today.

Nonetheless, the two were opposites in many ways. On one side, radicality, autonomy, identity, liberty; on the other, a vaguely audacious kind of conformity. On one side, sensuality, desire, pleasure; on the other, sexuality, lust, arousal. On one side, delectation; on the other, consummation. On one side, true provocation; on the other, mere teasing.

At *Vogue*, Francine Clement became Bourdin's regular collaborator. It was she who introduced him to the shoe designer Roland Jourdan in 1964. So began the great era of the Charles Jourdan brand, which ended in 1981, only to start up again, once more for Roland Jourdan, in the form of campaigns for Roland Pierre.

Long relationships with *Vogue* (thirty-three years) and Roland Jourdan (twenty-two years) gave rise to images that were unprecedented, unclassifiable, almost indescribable, with an apparent simplicity that masks layers of complexity.

'Linked on the surface by their functions within advertising and the fashion industry, his images are far more deeply connected by their constant exploration of the dream state, in all its possible aspects: erotic, mocking, cruel, elegant, disturbing,' wrote Luc Santé in his foreword to *Exhibit A* (2001).

Over time, Guy Bourdin became recognized as a master colourist. But while colour in photography often halts the eye and blocks the

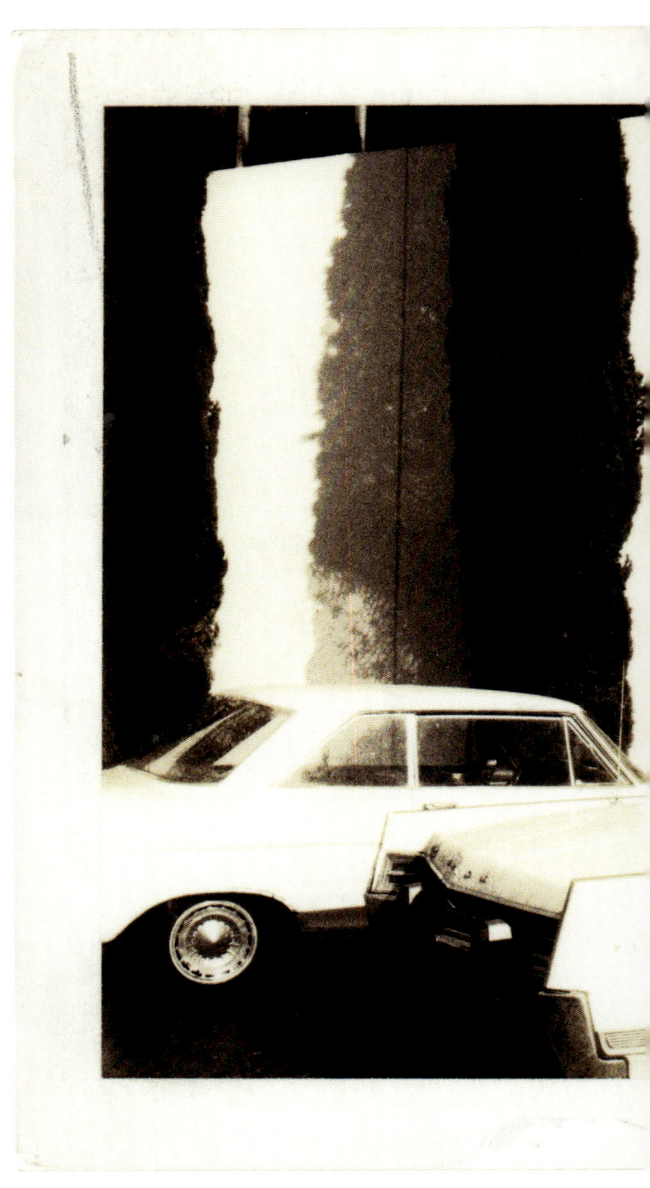

3. Guy Bourdin Archives, January 1978.

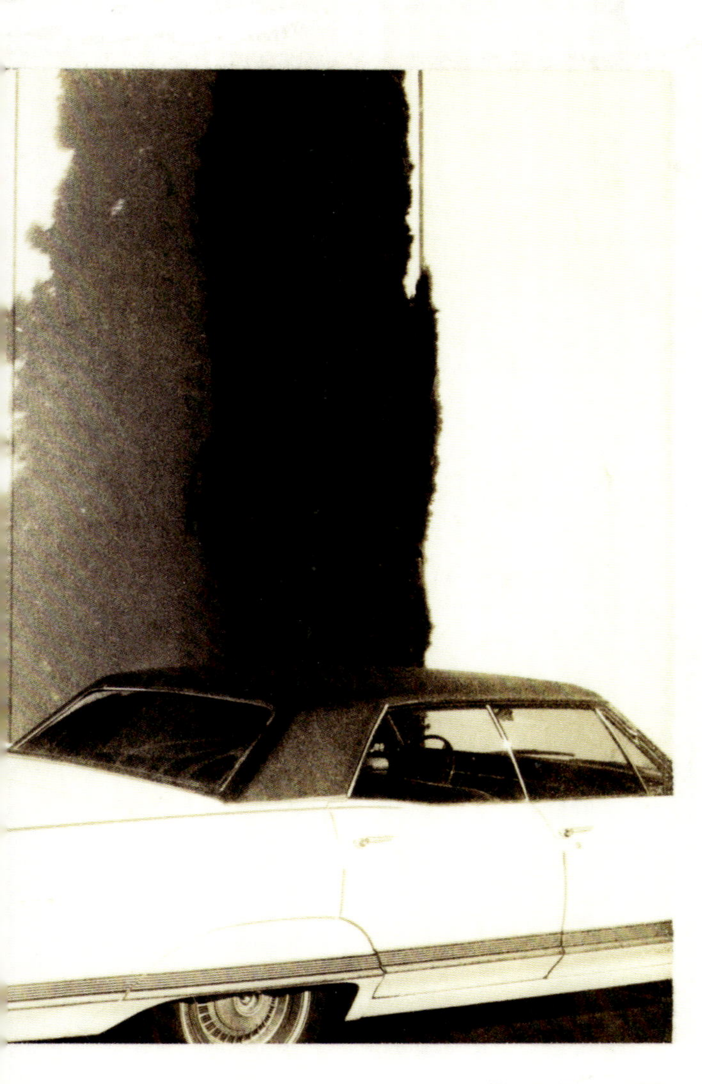

gaze, in his work it opens up space and the imagination. Speaking of his use of colours, the alternation between iciness and effervescence, and the omnipresence of bright, blood-red marks (or are they stains?), Alison M. Gingeras writes: 'In this way, Bourdin anticipates by more than a decade the work of such filmmakers as John Woo or Takeshi Kitano, who conflate highly stylized enactments of graphic violence with "painterly" gestures – saturating the frame with obviously fallacious representation of red blood.'

Although Sarah Moon, as an attentive observer of Bourdin's work, speaks of 'still cinema', and although filmmakers from David Lynch onwards seem to have seen and studied his images, Bourdin's work now leads us away from the cinema and into the realm of art. His large expanses of colour recall the Color Field paintings of Mark Rothko and Barnett Newman, while his bold, sharp lines recall the Hard Edge painting of Ellsworth Kelly. More easily, perhaps, because of the figurative nature of his work, one might associate him with the dreamlike geometry of Giorgio de Chirico, the dark humour of René Magritte, often caustic and cruel with a tendency to be morbid, or even Edward Hopper, whose fixed landscapes, hotel rooms and solitary figures all resonate with Bourdin's imagery.

Homages to Magritte and Hopper can be found throughout Bourdin's body of work, as well as nods to Hitchcock, winks to Weegee, shadows of Steve Hiett and more. One could endlessly produce further clues, evaluate influences and inspirations, consider common ground, follow diverging paths and trace converging lines, but the conclusion would always be the same: Bourdin is outside, above and beyond photography.

In any case, he is certainly outside the usual mould of fashion photographers, although Paris still hums with a thousand anecdotes, and the fashionistas still mock the many 'moods' of the master, his demands and foibles, which Magali Jauffret describes so beautifully: '...keeping Ursula Andress sprawled on a glass table for six hours, waiting for someone to track down some roses in exactly the right shade to match her skin tone; the 500-million-franc diamond tossed into a pot of paint; the frantic opening of forty different cans of peas to find one that was his favourite shade of bright green...'[1]

Fashion and advertising, with *Vogue* and Charles Jourdan in the
vanguard, but also *Harper's Bazaar* and *20 ans*, and Claude Montana
and Issey Miyake, Chanel and Ungaro, Bloomingdale's and Révillon,
Pentax and Yashica, and more.

Then the Grand Prix National de la Photographie, awarded
in 1985 by the French Ministry of Culture (which he refused but
which still stands in any case), and the Infinity Award in 1988,
from the ICP in New York, presented to him by Annie Leibowitz.

Then in 2003, twelve years after his death, international
recognition, thanks to the enthusiasm and commitment of Shelly
Verthime, in the form of his first major retrospective exhibition
at the Victoria & Albert Museum in London, an exhibition that would
later travel to the National Gallery of Victoria in Melbourne and the
Jeu de Paume in Paris.

Fashion and advertising, that is how the art world saw him. An artist,
that is how the smaller world of fashion and advertising saw him.
For once, it was the second of these worlds that saw the situation best.
Elsewhere, this fact has not yet granted Bourdin the status he deserves,
the status of an artist who was unique, autonomous and ultimately,
as indescribable as he was seductive.

Was Bourdin really a surrealist (or post-surrealist), as he is often
called? At the very beginning, of course, he admired Man Ray and
went to visit him, and in turn was welcomed and listened to, and
given a letter of recommendation. Then, of course, he paid homage
to Magritte. Then, of course, there are these words from André
Breton: 'It is impossible for me to see a picture as anything other than
a window, and my first concern is always to find out what can be seen
through it.' Words that fit Bourdin aptly, among many others.

Beyond surrealism, it is the baroque that we think of, so
enraptured are we by the astonishing succession of movements
and contrasts, stretched and twisted shapes, broken-up perspectives,
curves and rhythms, illusions and emotions, heroism and sensuality,
voluptuous ecstasy and knowing ambiguity.

In both Bourdin's art and the art of the baroque, there is a
ceaseless search for beauty, by any possible means; beauty as a pretext

4. Moscow, 1959.

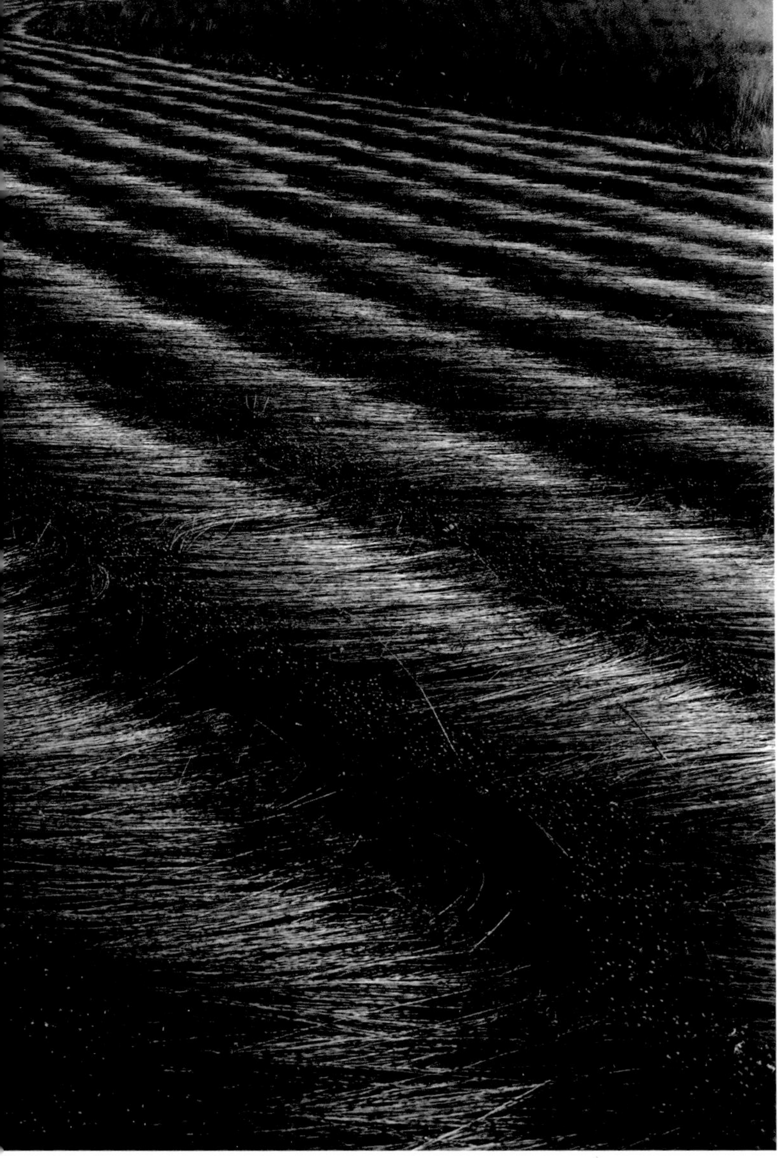

for and guarantee of ecstasy. To call this baroque emphasizes elegance and impertinence, motion and lightness, vertigo and illusion.

When we consider the life and work of Guy Bourdin, how can we help thinking of other artists, just as singular and unique as he?

Domenico Gnoli, for example, who is also considered a child of surrealism, and with whom he shares a cinematic sense of staging and silence. Both play with the concepts of enigma, absence, timeless stillness, impenetrability. Both use body parts, body masks, body places. And the same angelic face!

Or Francis Bacon, and not only because of the utter chaos of their studios, nor for their legacy of bags full of rubbish, nor for the flayed meat in 'Chapeaux-Choc'.

Or David Hockney, for his passion for Polaroids for one thing, but also for their obvious shared love of swimming pools: *Sunbather* (1966), *A Bigger Splash* (1968), *Rubber Ring Floating in a Swimming Pool* (1971), and *Portrait of an Artist (Pool with Two Figures)* (1971) are all reflected in Bourdin's own series of pools (1975–78).

Or Balthus, for their shared interest in models who are young, fresh, slim and supple. 'I see adolescent girls as a symbol. I could never paint a woman. The beauty of adolescence is more interesting. Adolescence embodies the future, existence before perfect beauty arrives. A woman has already found her place in the world, a teenage girl has not. The body of a woman is already complete. The mystery has gone,' said Balthus. One can easily imagine Bourdin feeling the same way when one day there arrived at his house an unknown seventeen-year-old, Nicolle Meyer, vaguely a model, accomplished as a dancer, dreaming of music, still fragile and mysterious. A work that had yet to be completed, not a photograph to take.

Or Robert Malaval, another flamboyant and unusual figure, with whom Bourdin shared a love of total freedom, the attitude of a dandy, the refusal to let his career overshadow his work. On the occasion of his exhibition *Poussière d'étoiles* ('Stardust') in 1974, Malaval wrote: 'it is well known that there is nothing more precious than that little heart that beats as she sleeps on the studio couch, I would give all the art in the universe for that, for this sublime and fragile thing, easy to inflame, easy to extinguish, just a spark of life...' In one of his many notebooks

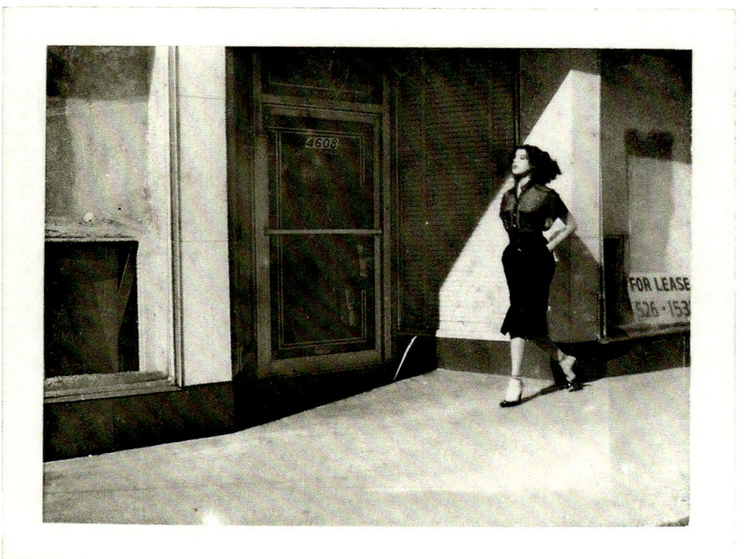

5. Guy Bourdin Archives, January 1978.

(he wrote, drew and painted as much as he photographed), Bourdin wrote: 'The emotions of my thoughts are so great that each thing that expresses beauty to me, each thing that crosses my path, I shall call by your name. So a tree that makes music will be you and every time that the space(?)/blue(?) reads I love you, that will be the way it is along my path, milestones marking my steps and the beats of my heart...'

Or Daniel Pommereulle, for whom 'nothing moves fast enough on the edge of death', so constant is the presence of death, the obsession with death, within the work of both of them. Eros and Thanatos, once again impossible to separate.

Trying to chart every feature of Guy Bourdin means coming up against his own library. Not just a library of photography or of art, but of essays and writings. To begin, Giorgio Agamben: 'Each time, we have to wrench back from the mechanisms the possibility of usage they have taken captive. The profanation of the unprofanable is the political task of the coming generation.'

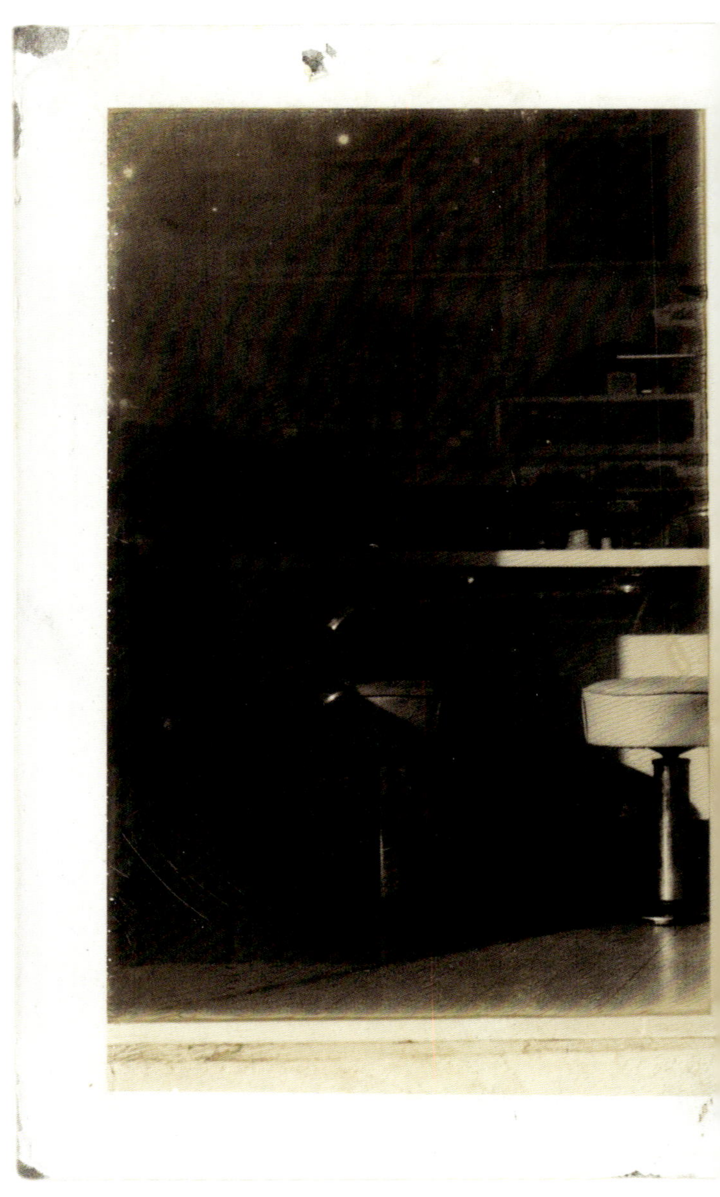

6. Guy Bourdin Archives, January 1978.

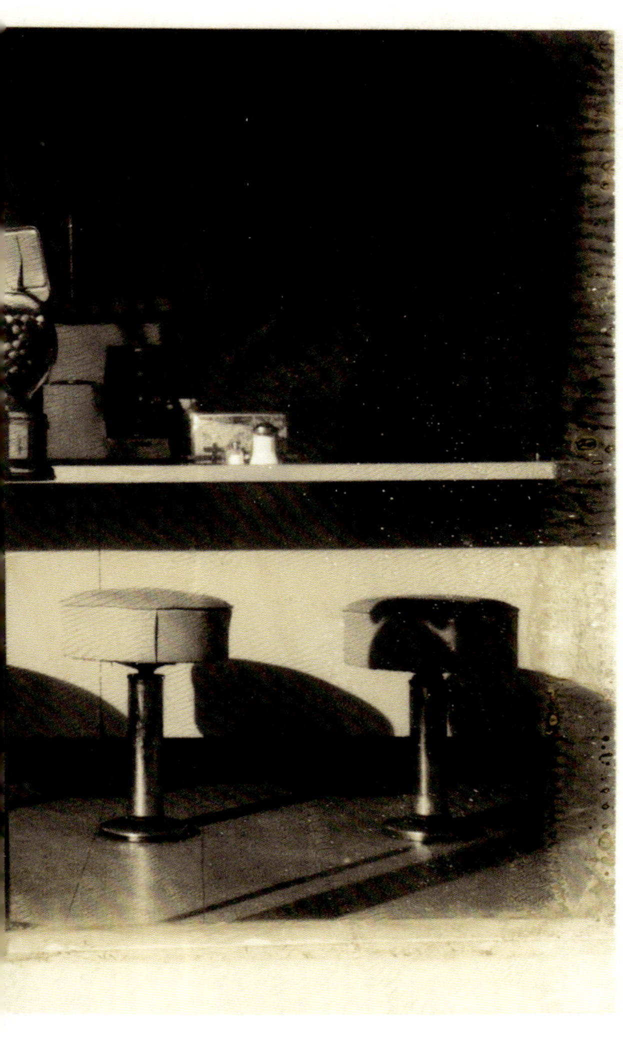

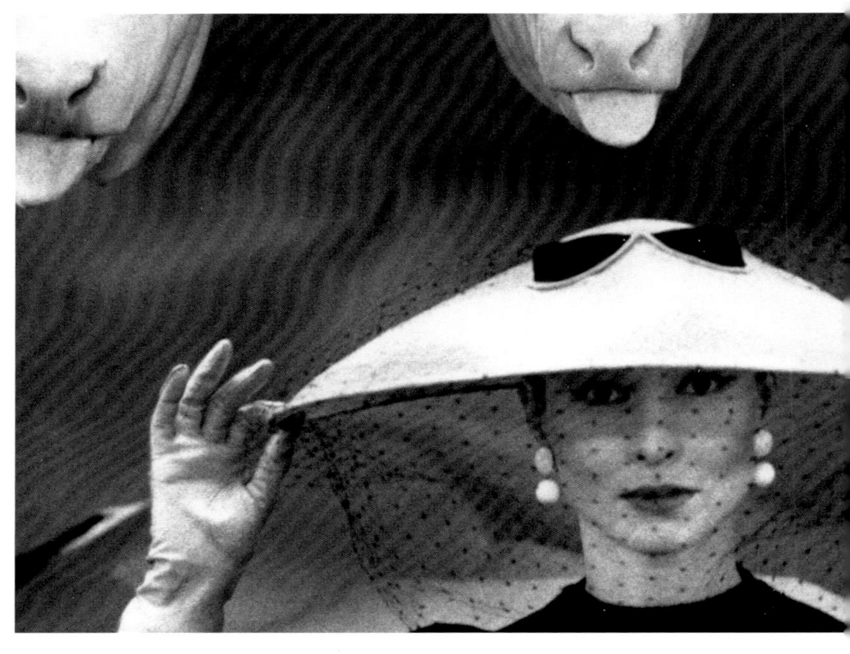

7. 'Chapeaux-Choc', *Vogue France*, hat by Claude Saint-Cyr, February 1955.

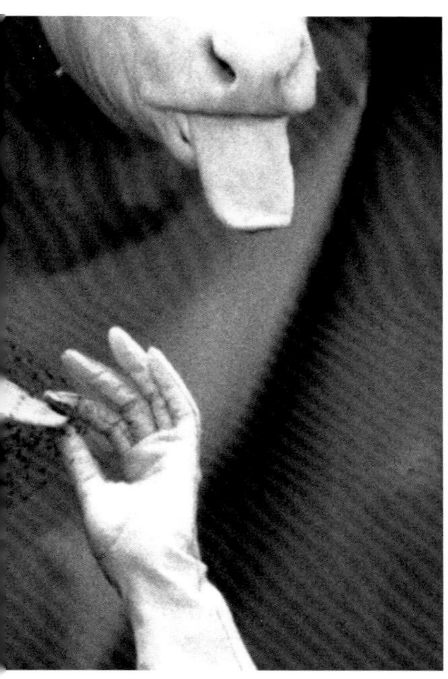

To continue, Michelangelo Antonioni: 'We know that under the developed image lies another that is more faithful to reality, and under that, yet another, and so on. Until we come to the image of absolute and mysterious reality, that no one will ever see.'

To follow, Jean Baudrillard: 'Creating an image means stripping an object of all its dimensions, one by one: its weight, its texture, its scent, its depth, its time, its continuity and of course its meaning. This disembodiment, this exorcism, is the price paid to give the image its fascination and intensity.'

To conclude, Georges Didi-Hubermann: 'We demand too little of an image when we reduce it to a mere appearance. We demand too much of it when we seek reality itself inside it. What we need to do is to discover within it a capacity to make us rethink all of these things.'

Let us leave the paths of art and the roads of philosophy and return to photography alone. But which photograph, which register, which companions? Bourdin is an infinite universe, within which mingle the polychrome facts of a Helen Levitt or a William Eggleston, the stillness of a Jeff Wall or an Ed Ruscha, the mirroring and reflections of a John Baldessari or a Denis Roche, the conceptual yet surreal constructions of a David Buckland or a Victor Burgin, the shifting of a Cindy Sherman, the taste for the deadest of still lives of an Andres Serrano (incidentally, the Serrano Bar was one of his favourites), the skilful scene-setting (Sarah Moon's 'still cinema') of a Duane Michals.

One could go on endlessly, enumerating these meeting points and similarities and overlaps, without ever exhausting the mystery of Bourdin. Seducer and seductive, he certainly is. But above everything, impossible to sum up.

Gilles de Bure

Notes

1   Magali Jauffret, 'Guy Bourdin, l'œil absolu' in *Connaissance des Arts Photo*, no. 1, July/October 2004.

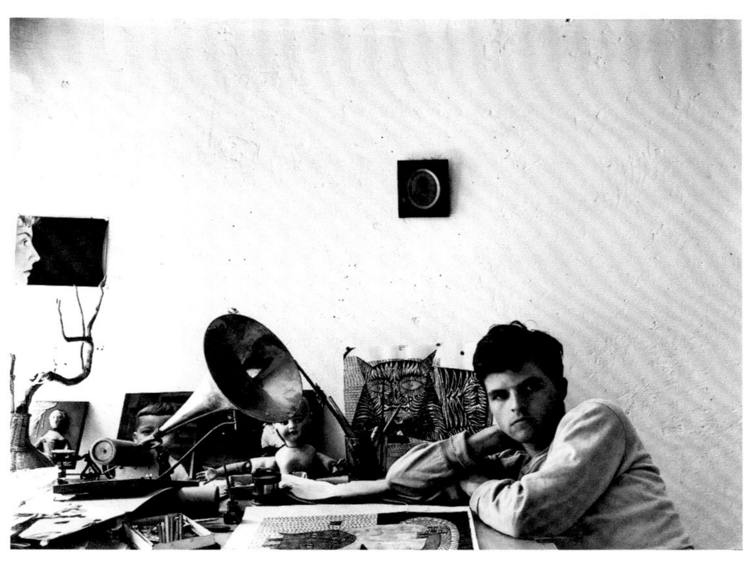

8. Self-portrait in the artist's studio, c. 1953–57.

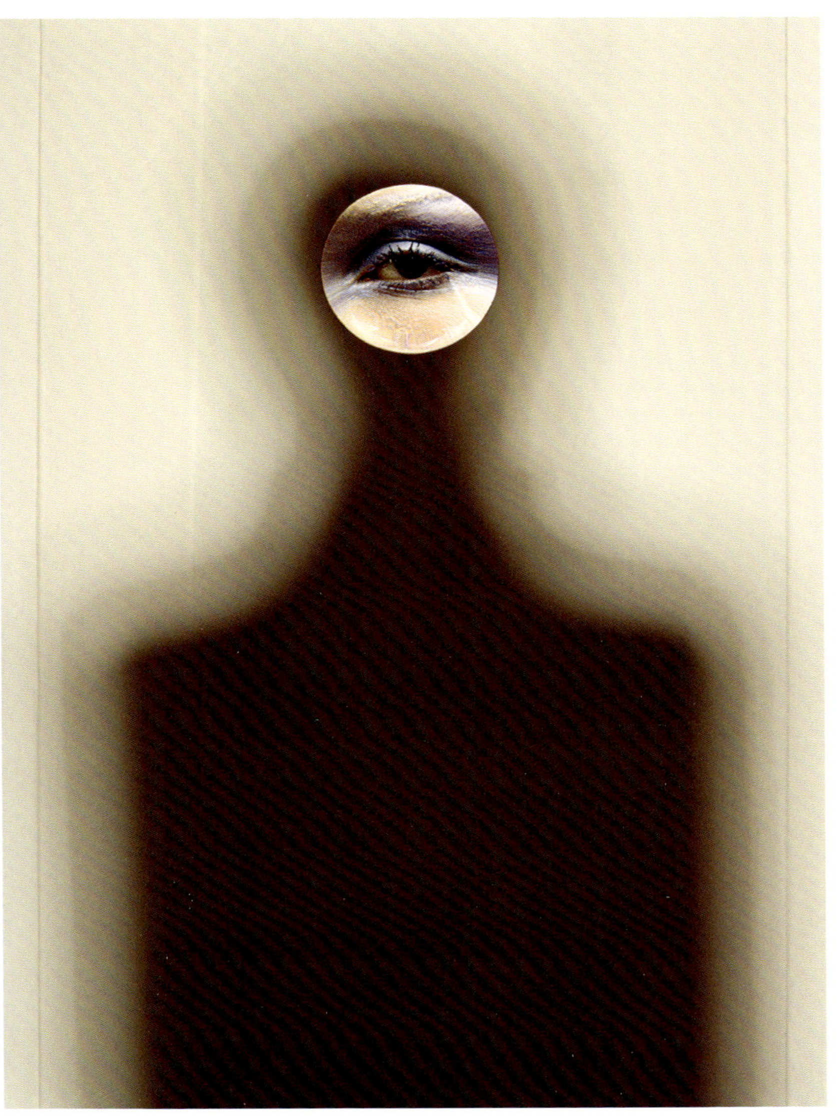

9. *Vogue France*, April 1972

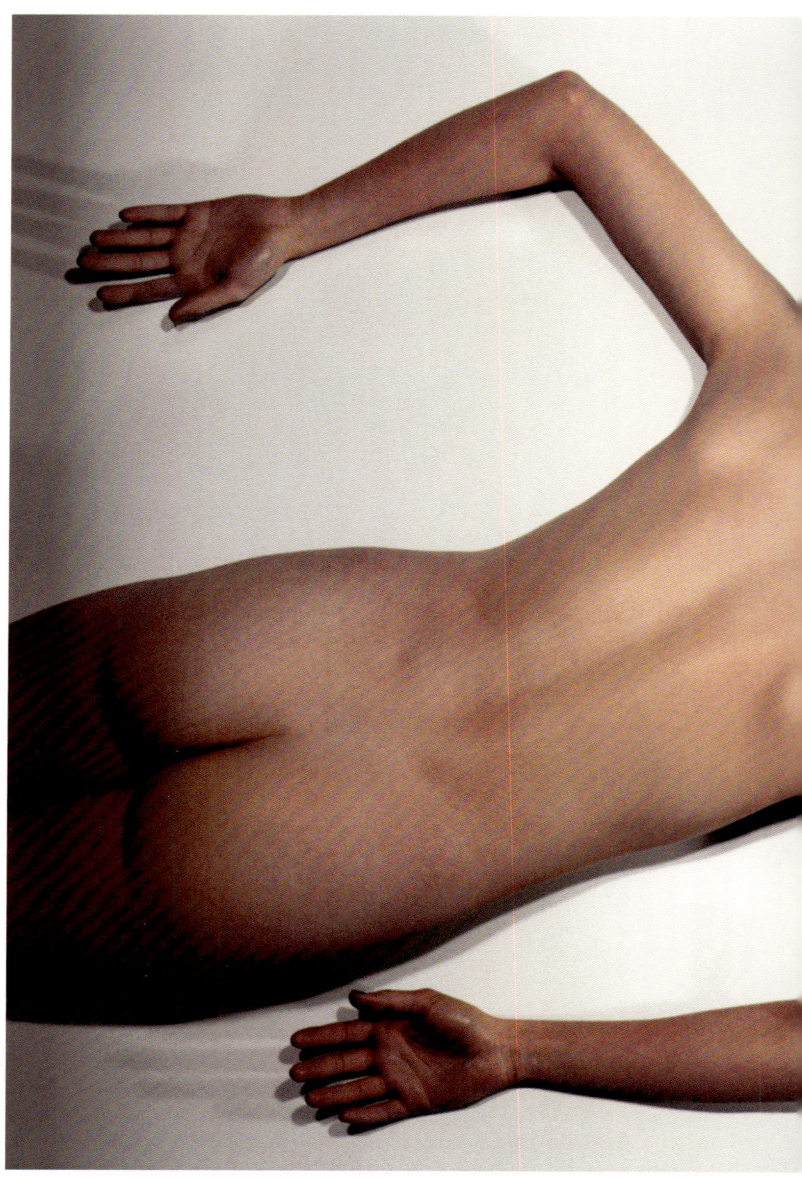

10. Pentax Calendar, 1980.

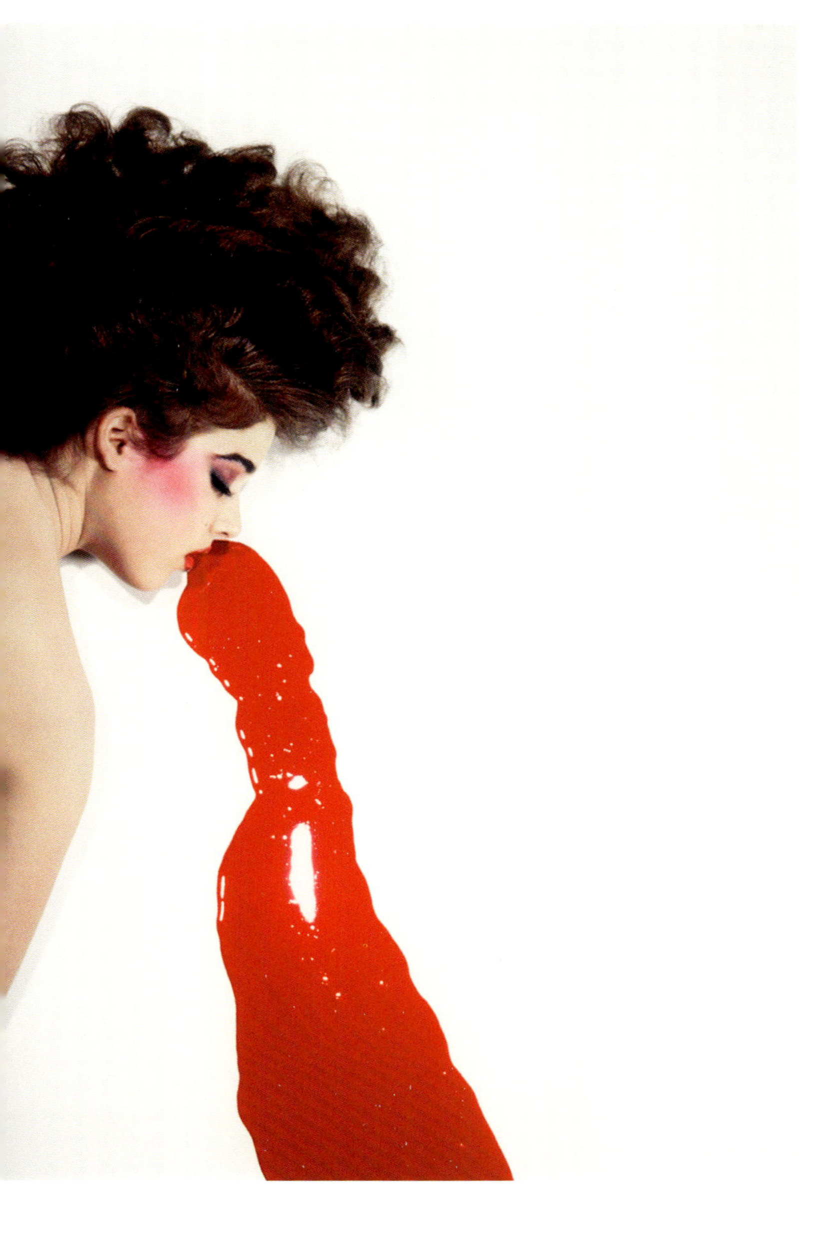

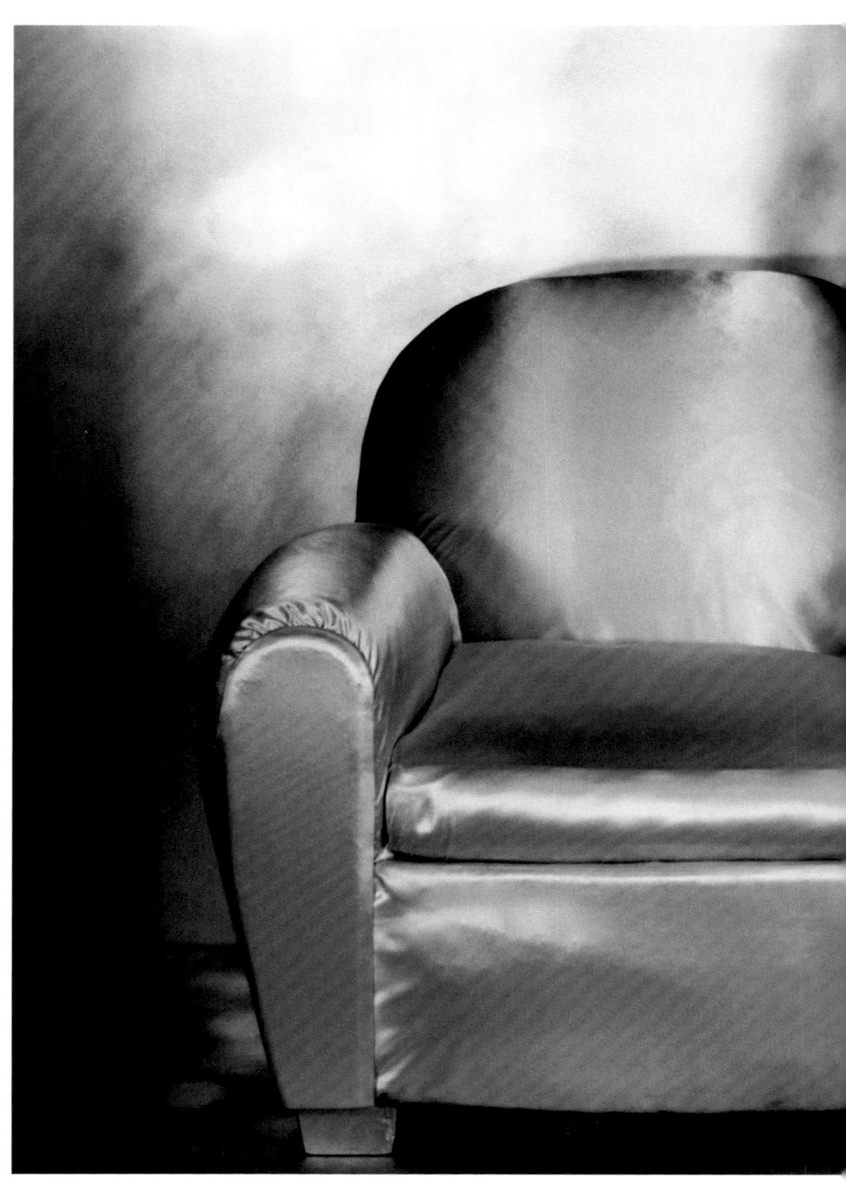

11. Guy Bourdin Archives, December 1979.

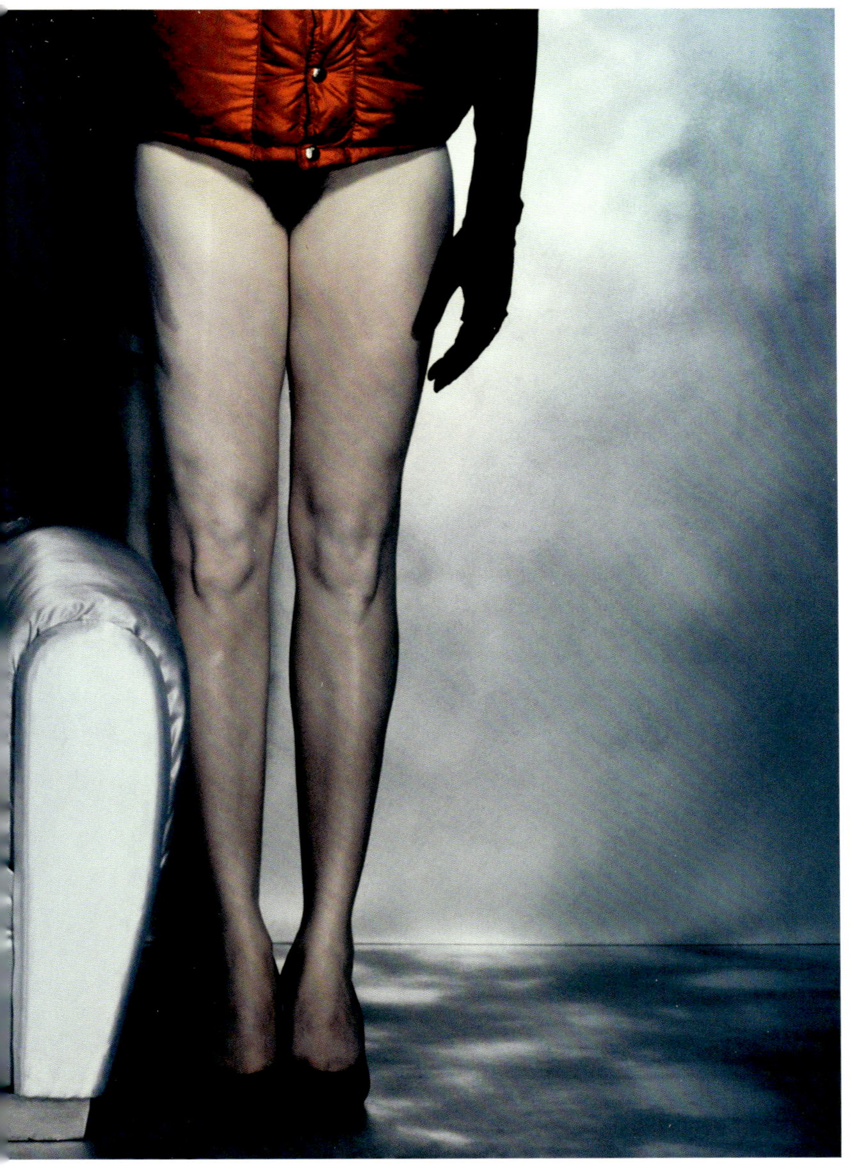

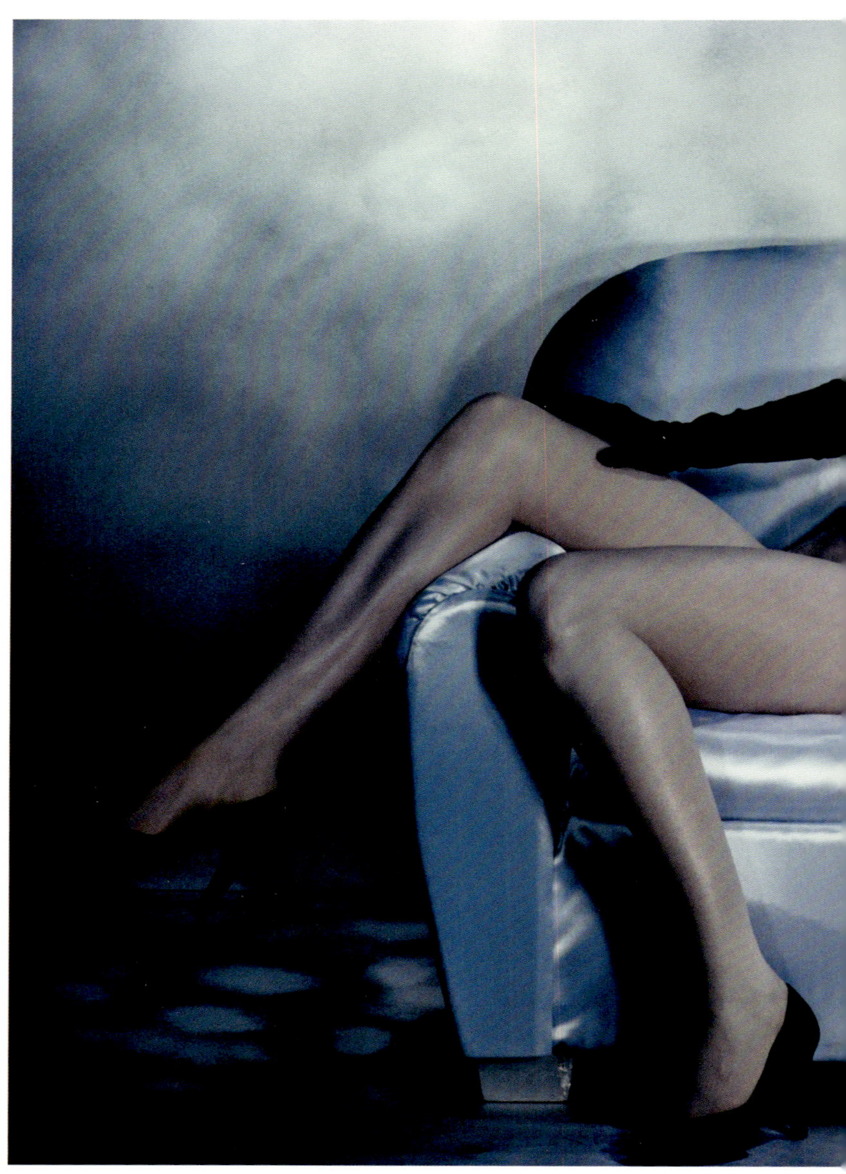

12. Pentax Calendar, 1980.

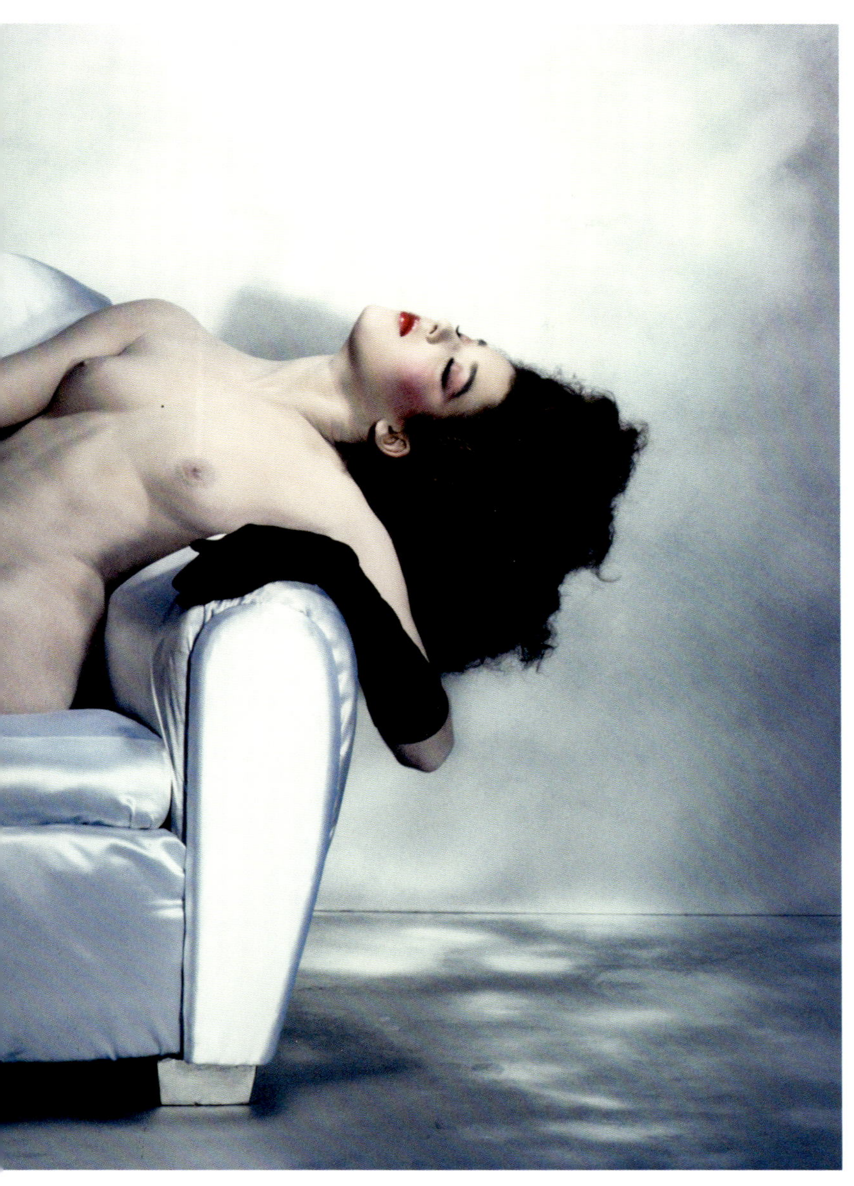

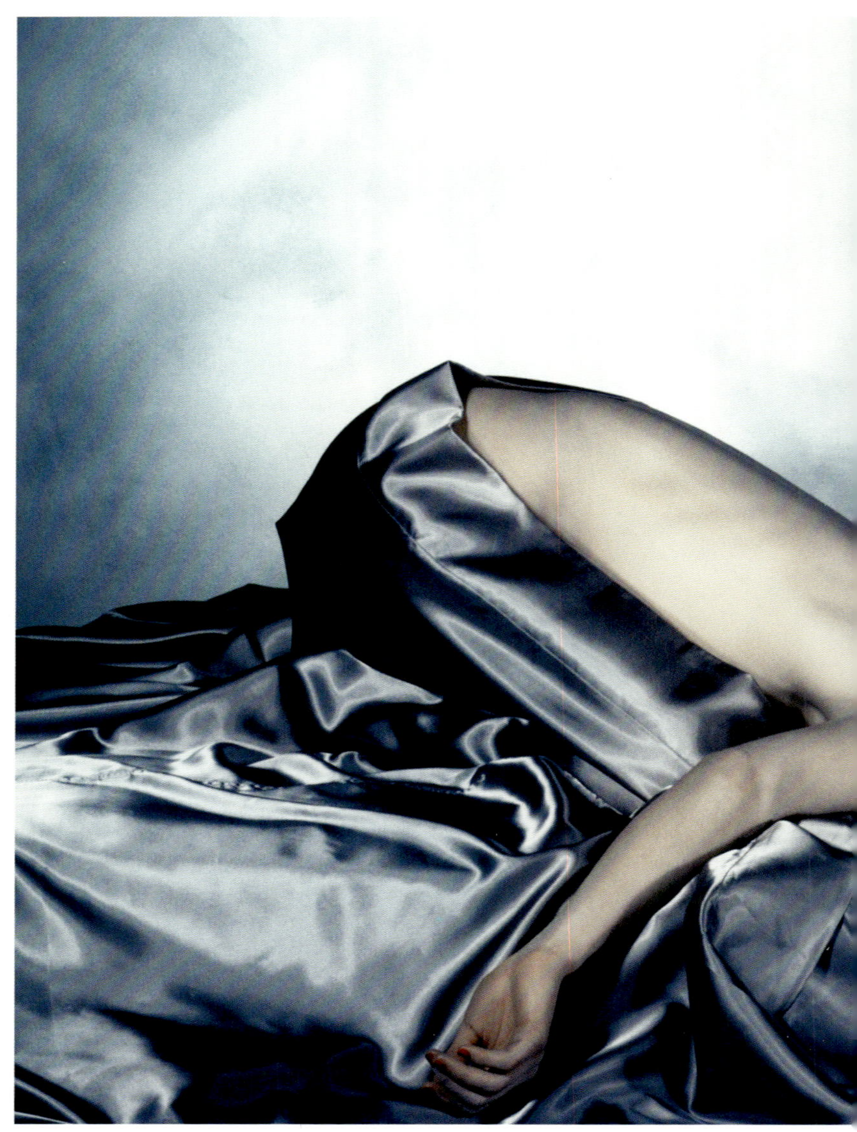

13. Pentax Calendar, 1980.

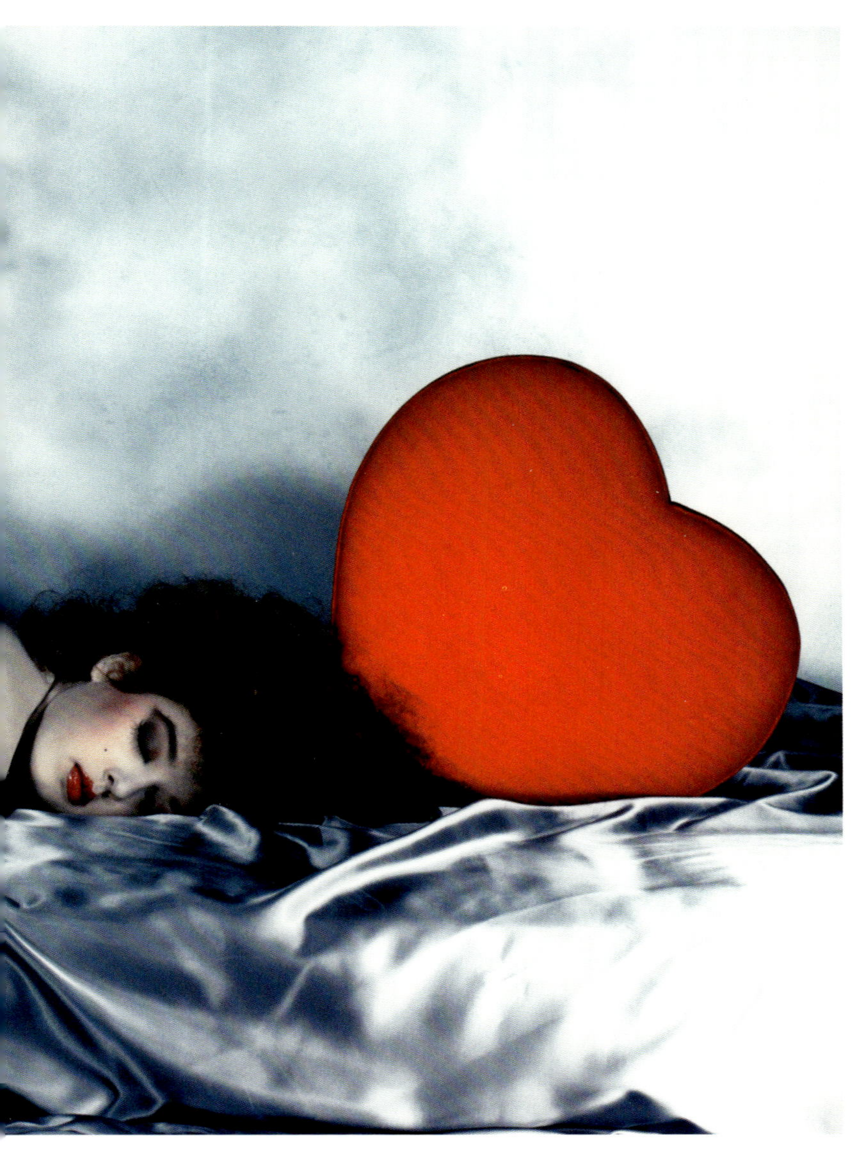

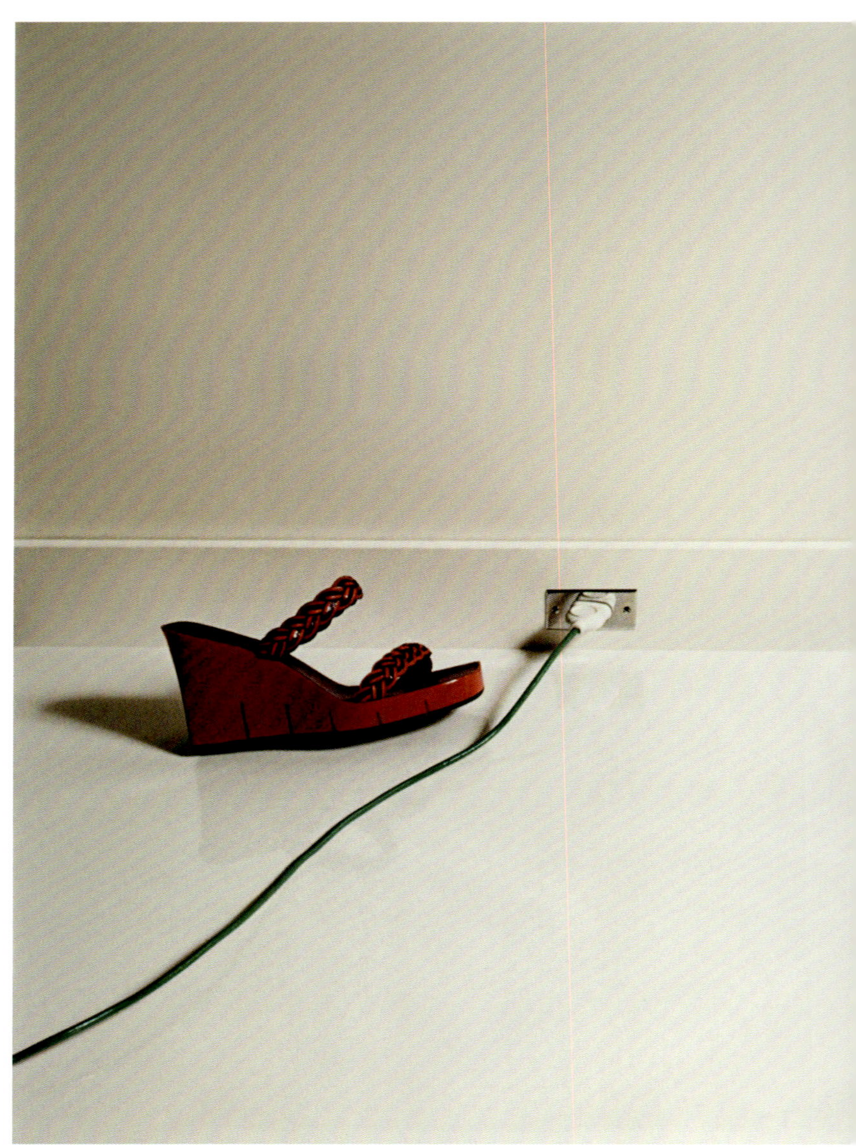

14. Campaign for Charles Jourdan, Spring 1975.

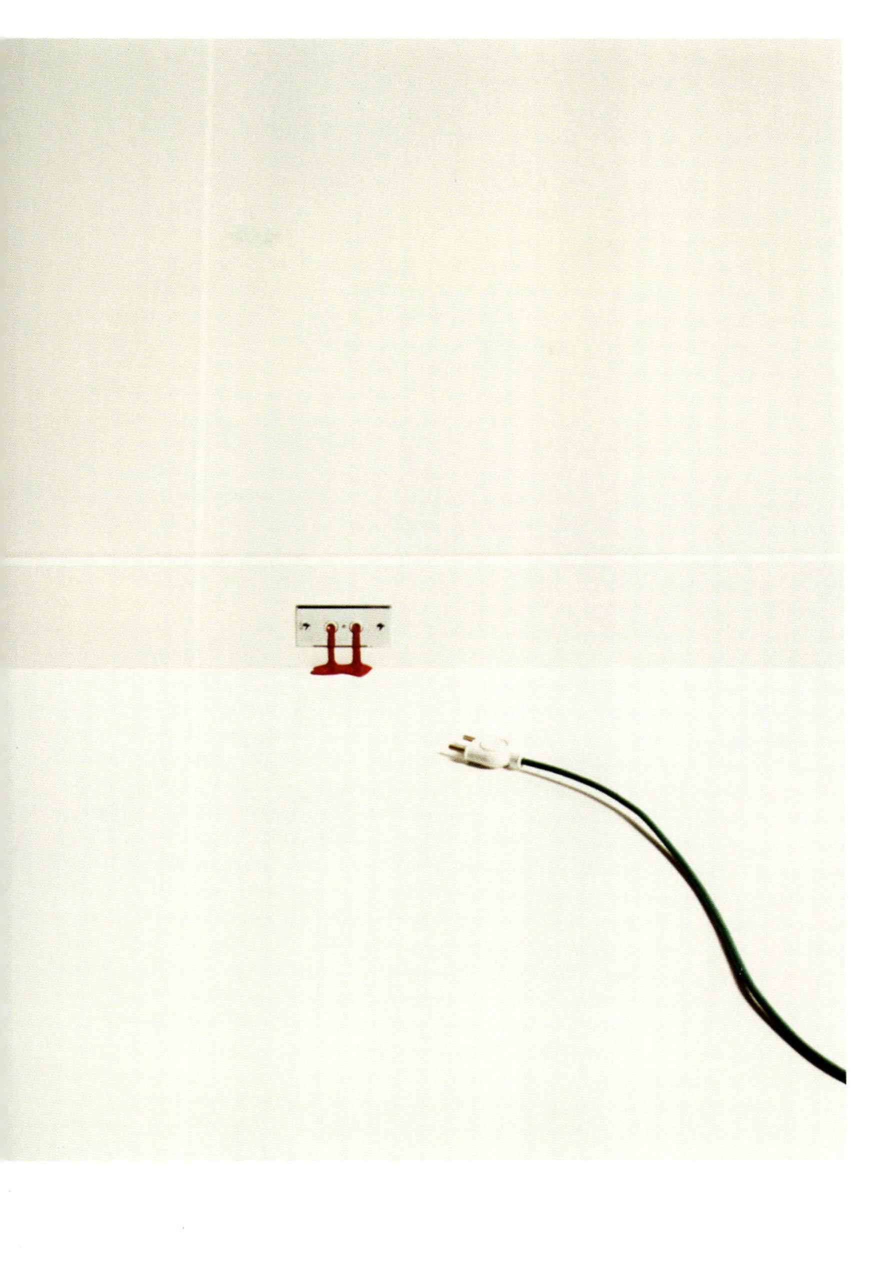

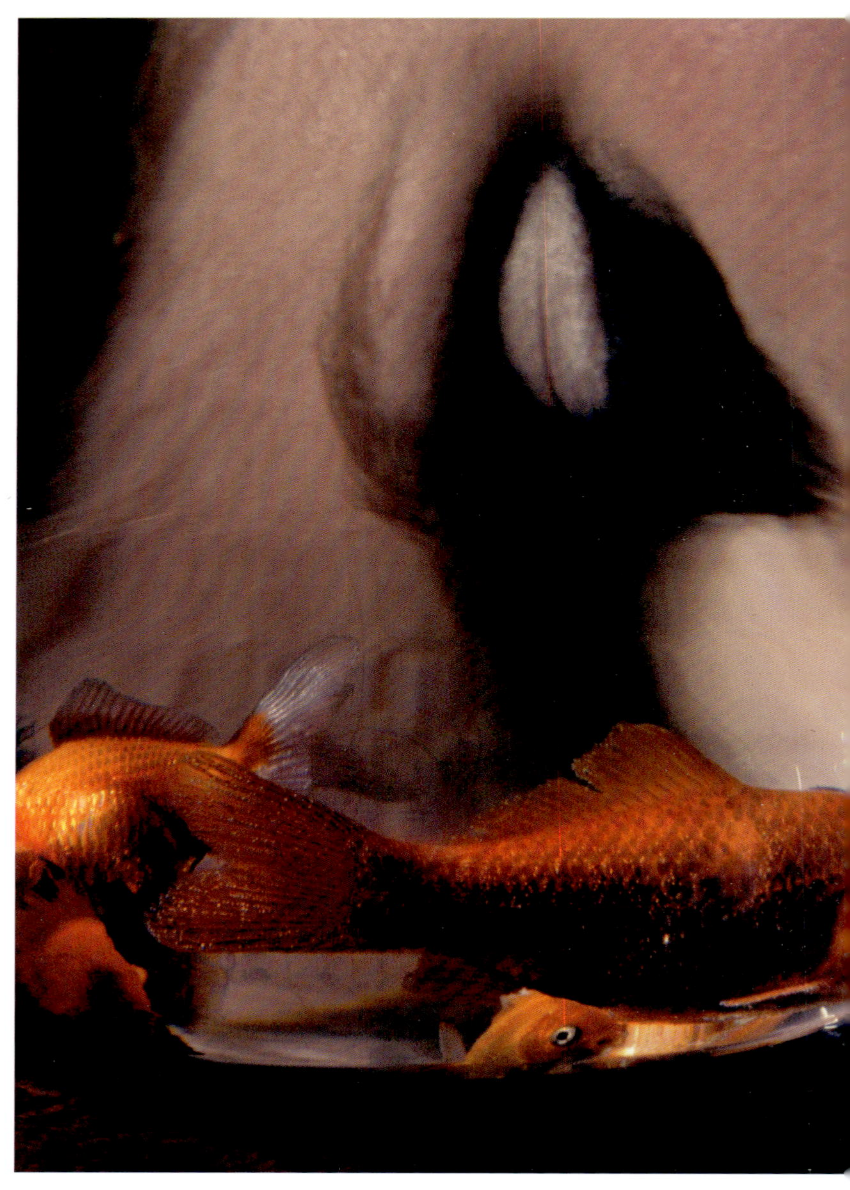

15. *Vogue France*, variant, May 1977.

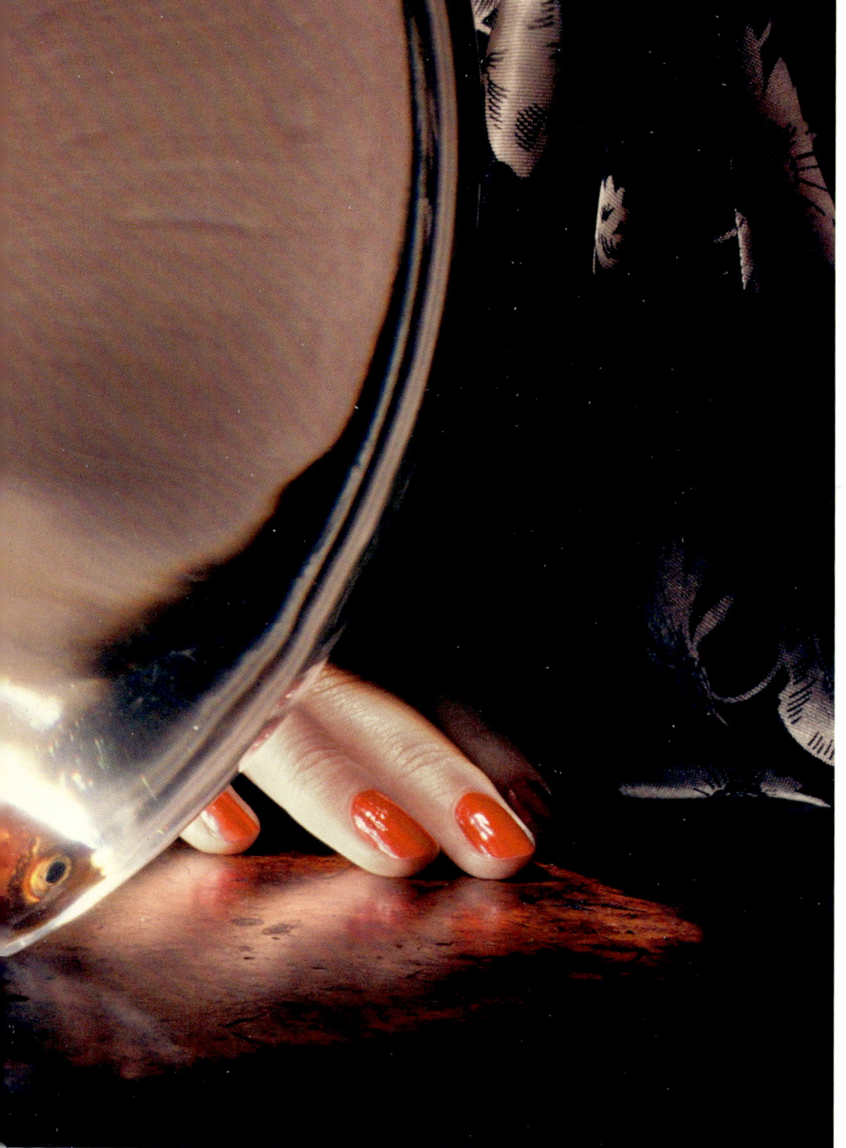

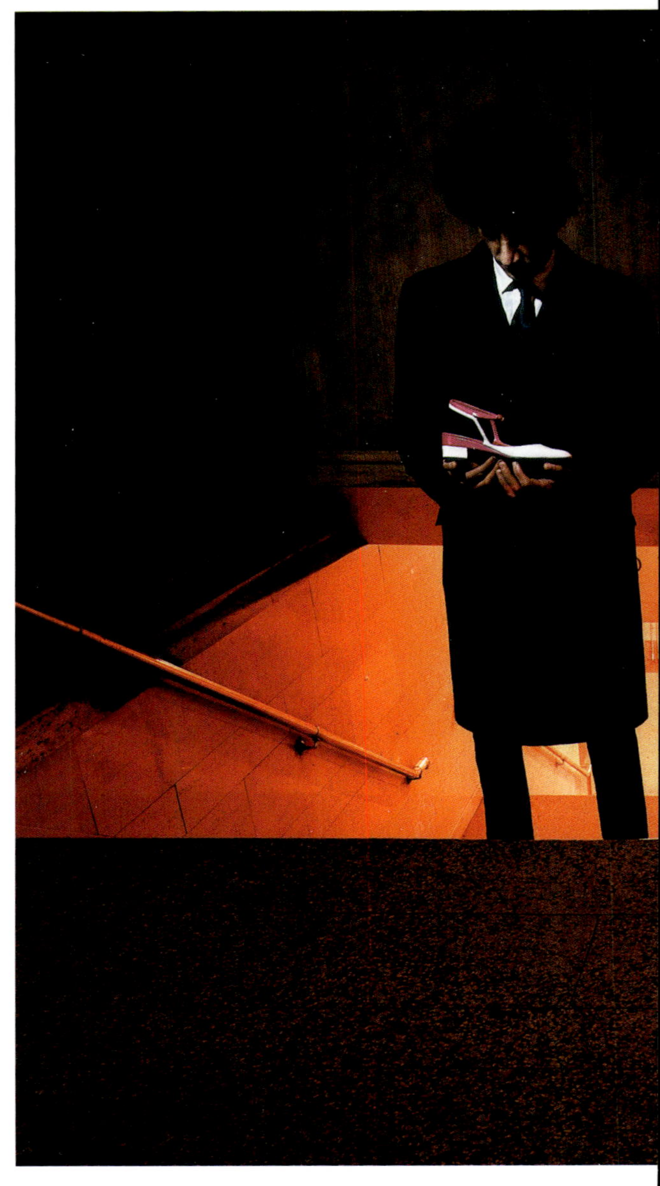

16. Campaign for Charles Jourdan, Spring 1968.

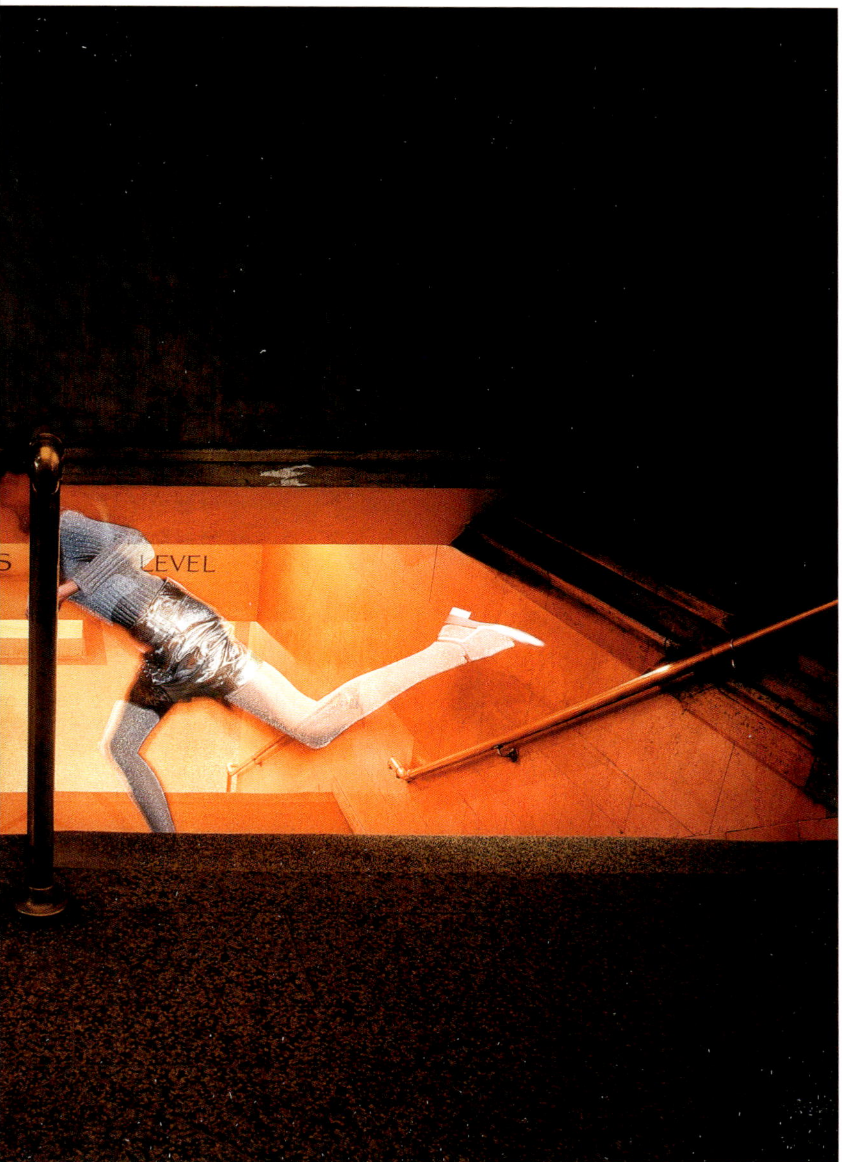
LEVEL

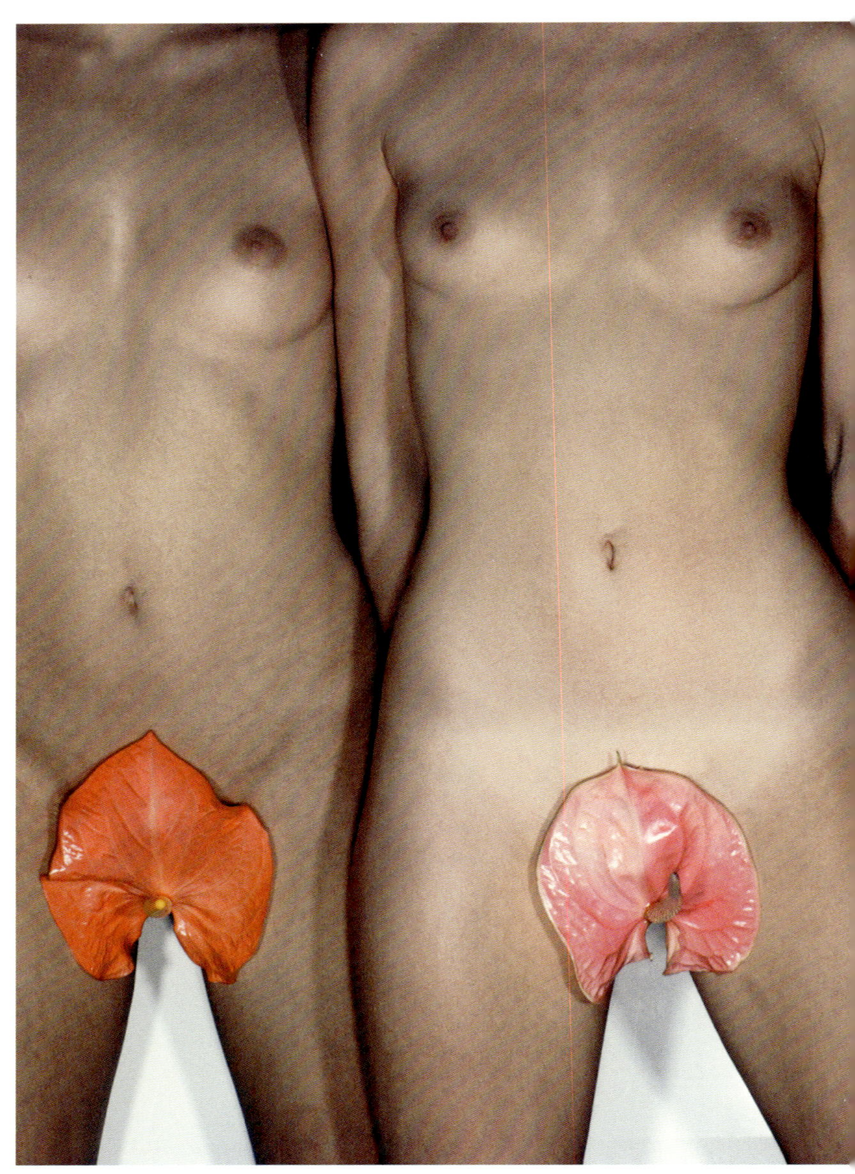

17. *Vogue France*, December 1976–January 1977.

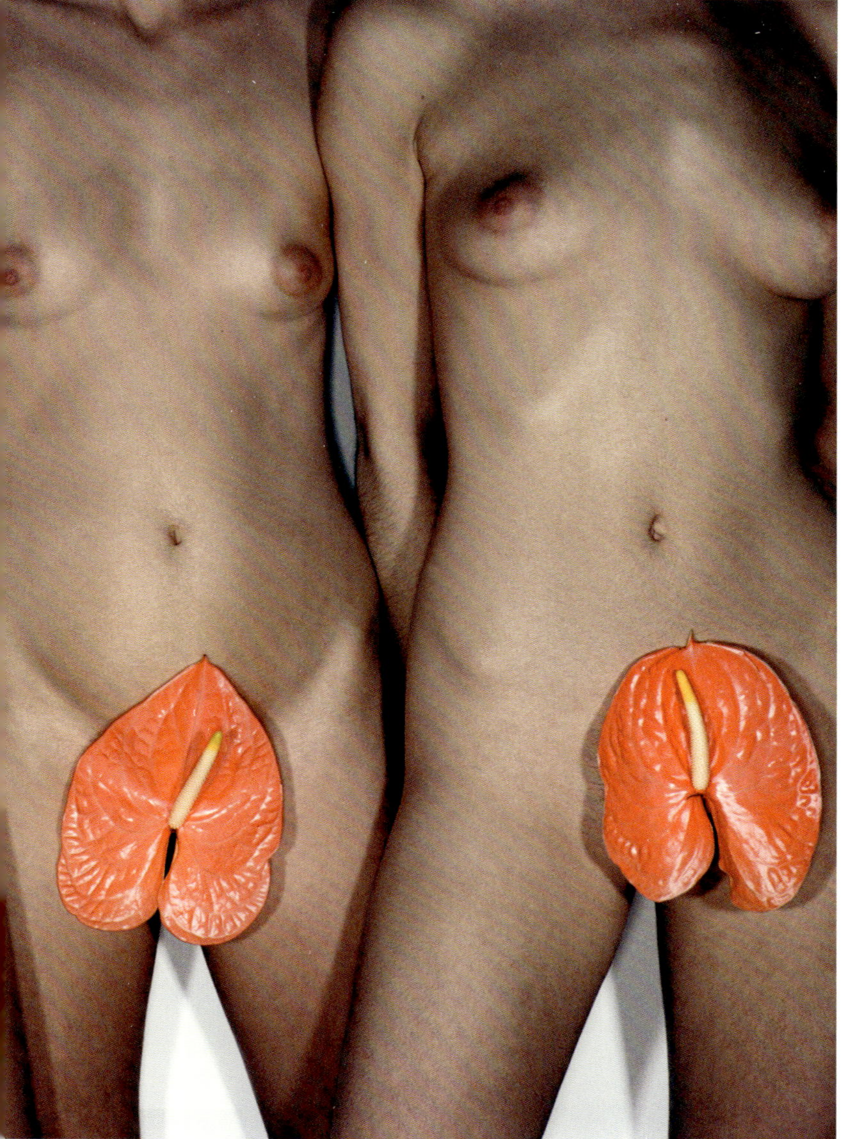

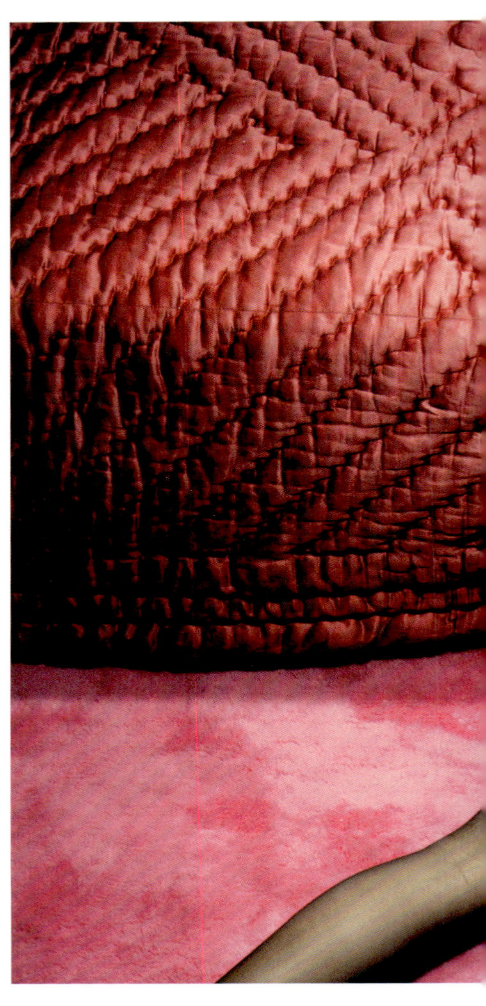

18. Pentax Calendar, 1980.

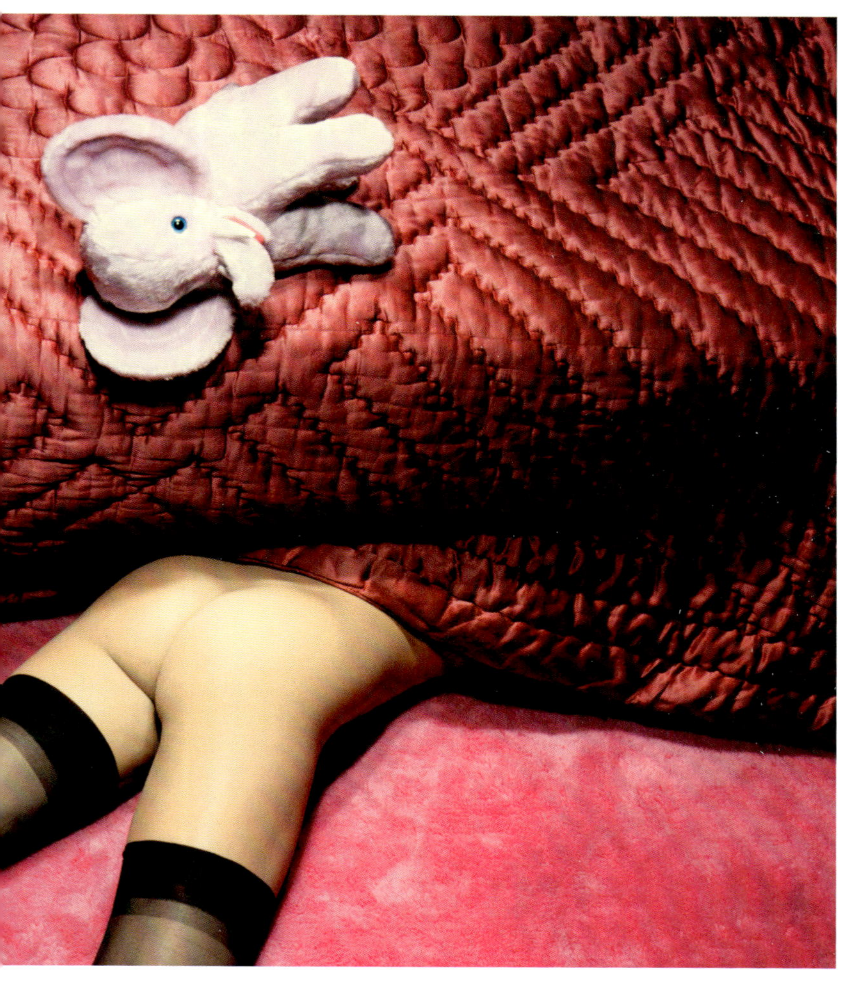

19. Campaign for Charles Jourdan, Spring 1979.

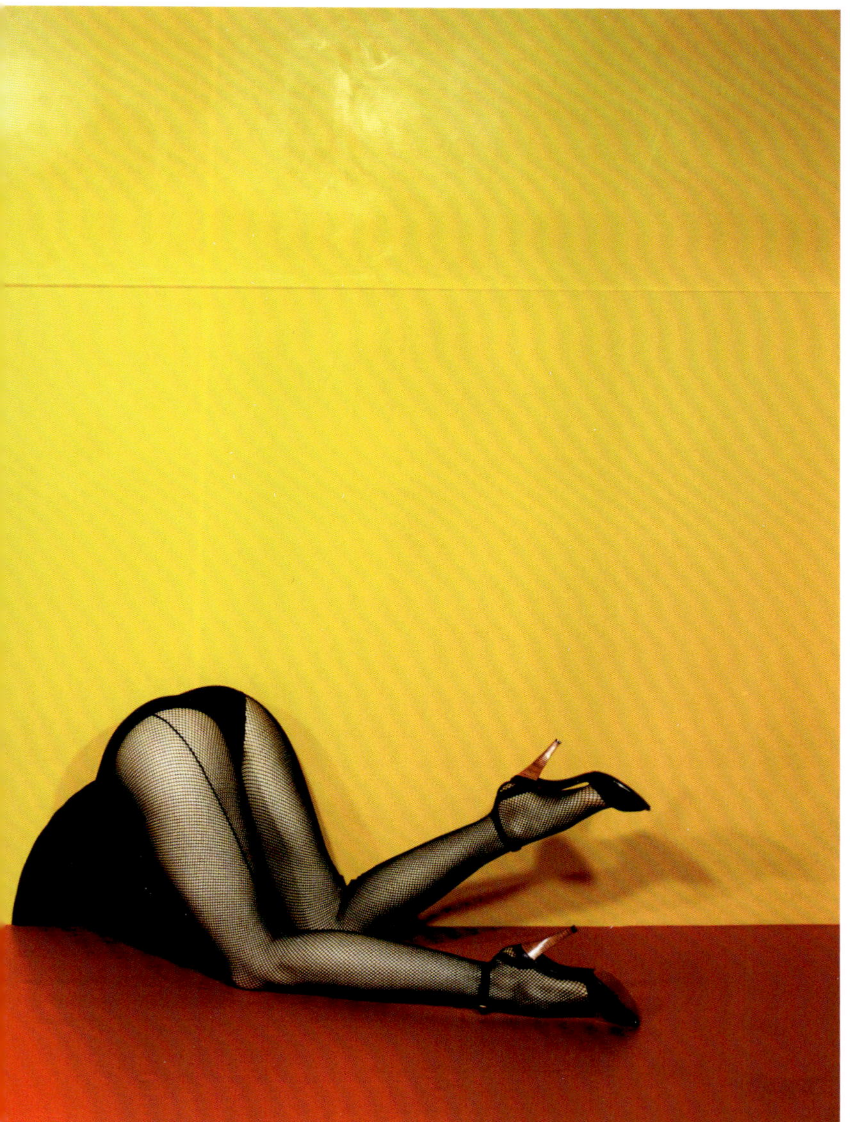

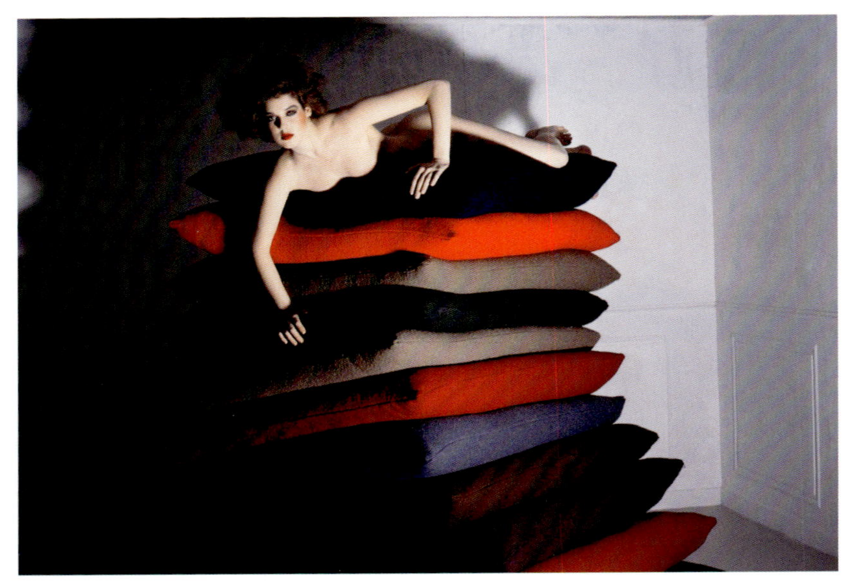

20. Guy Bourdin Archives, November 1977.

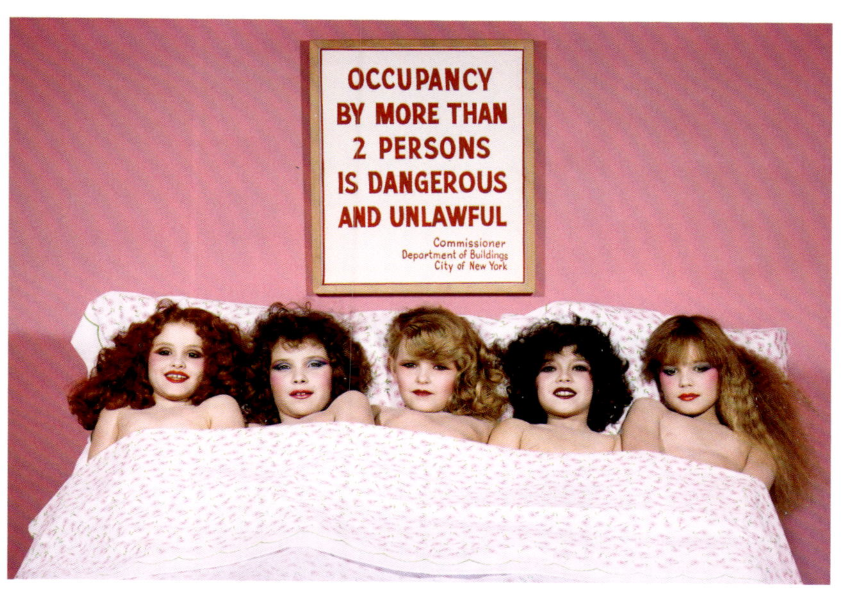

21. *Vogue France*, December 1977.

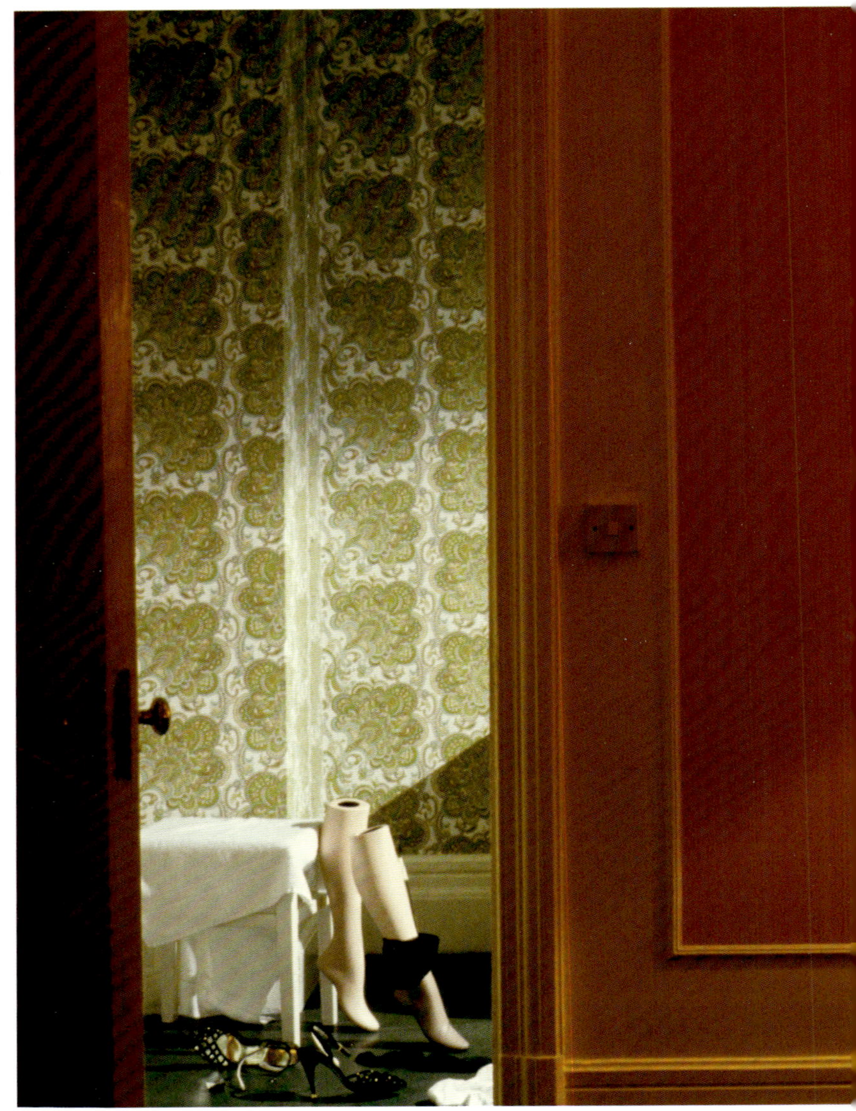

22. Campaign for Charles Jourdan, Autumn 1979.

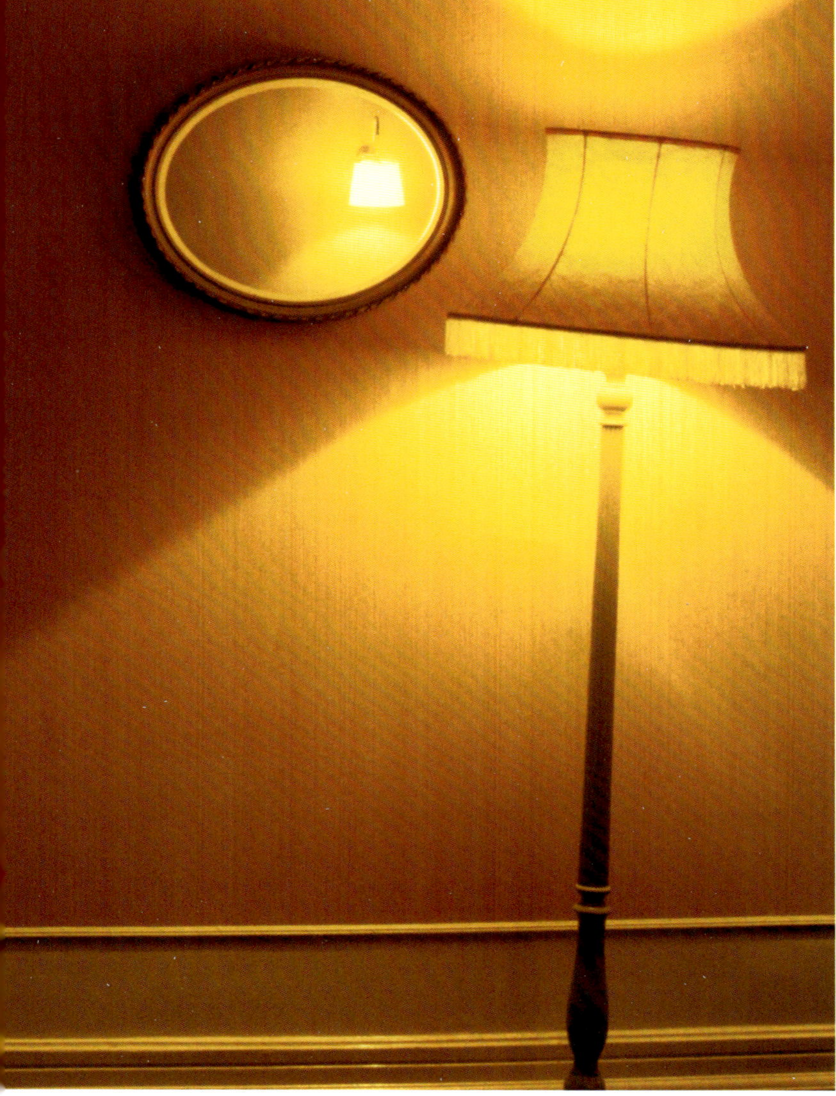

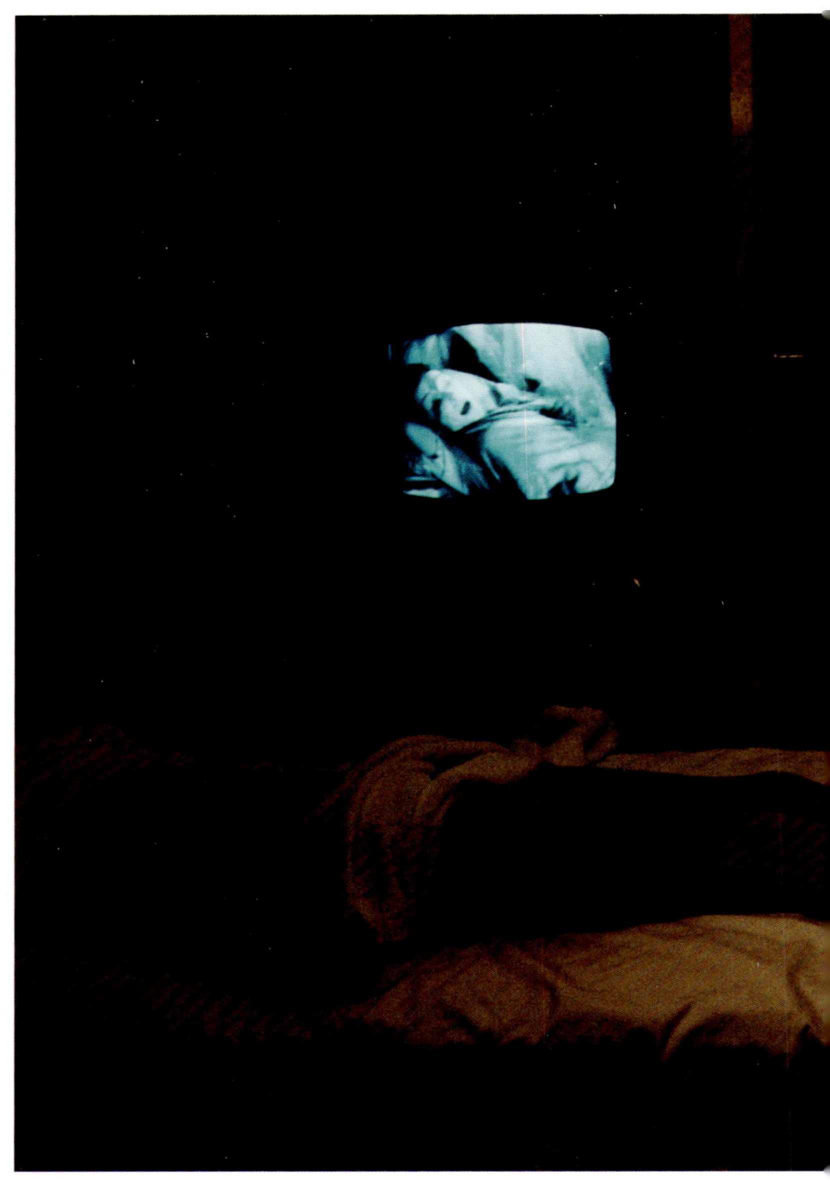

23. Campaign for Charles Jourdan, Spring 1975.

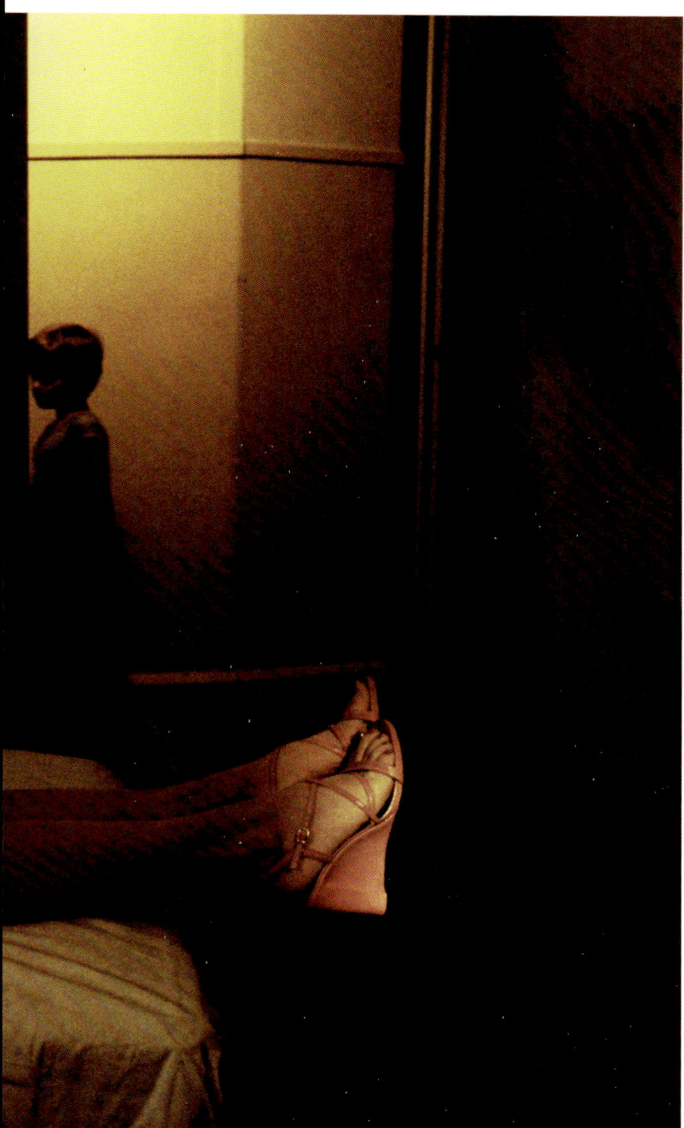

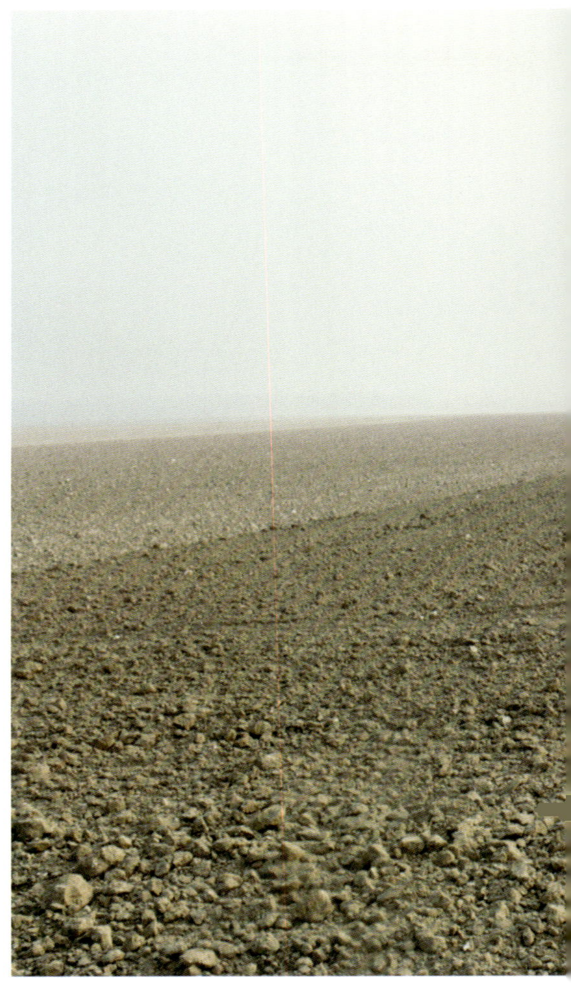

24. *Marie Claire France*, c. March–April 1980.

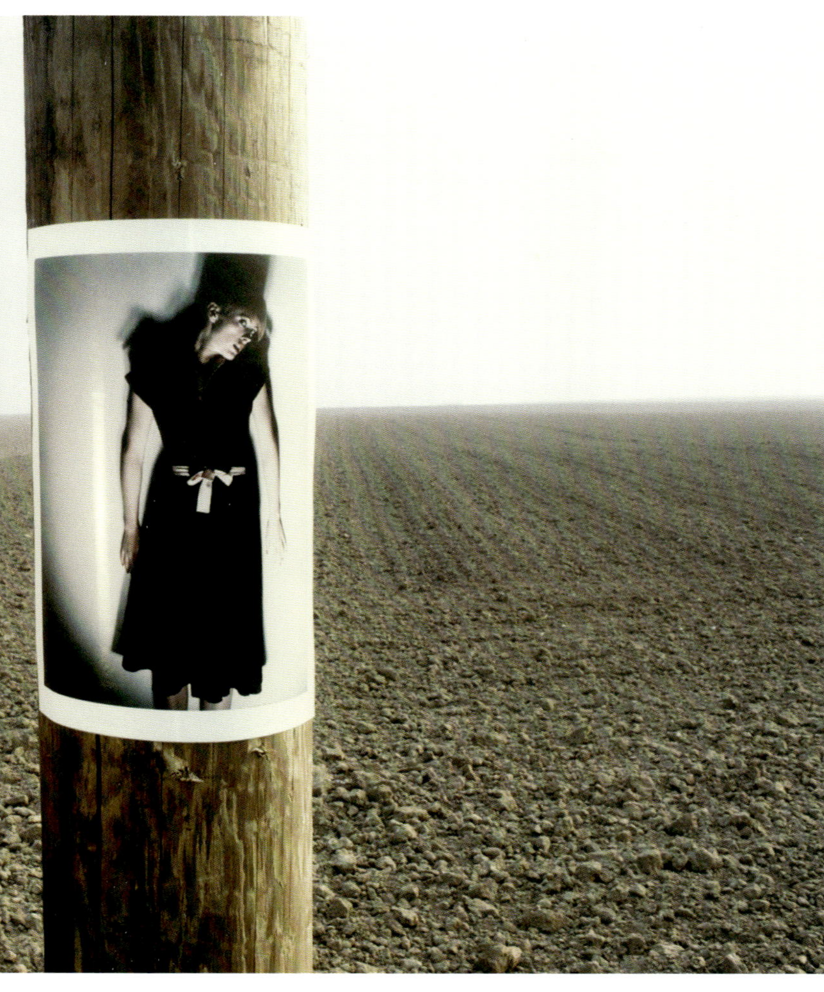

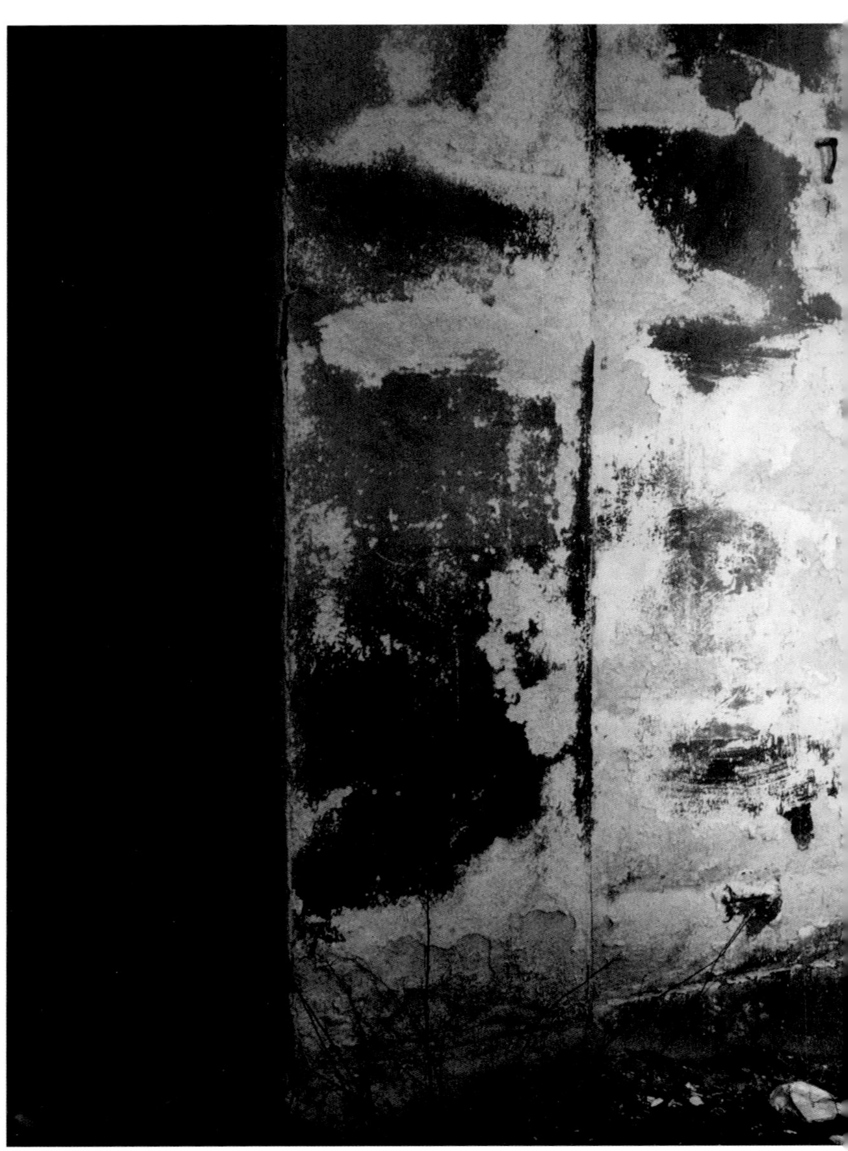

25. *Vogue France*, March 1976.

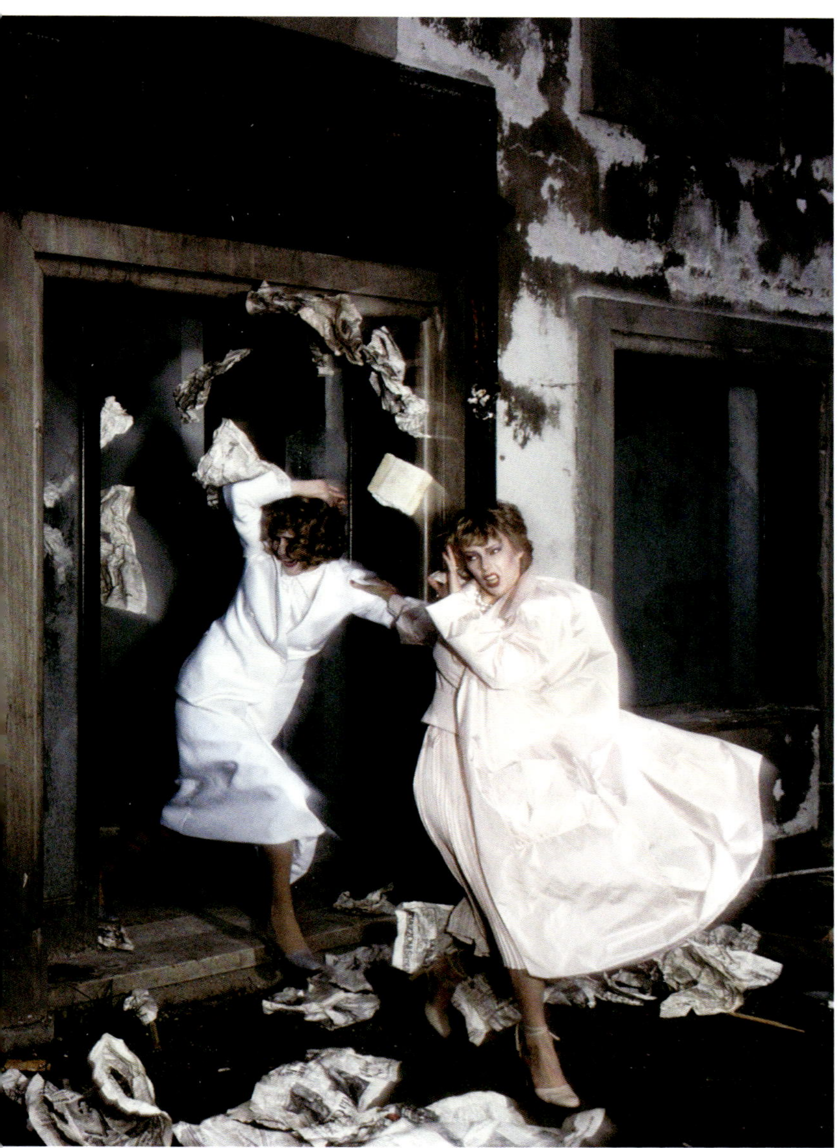

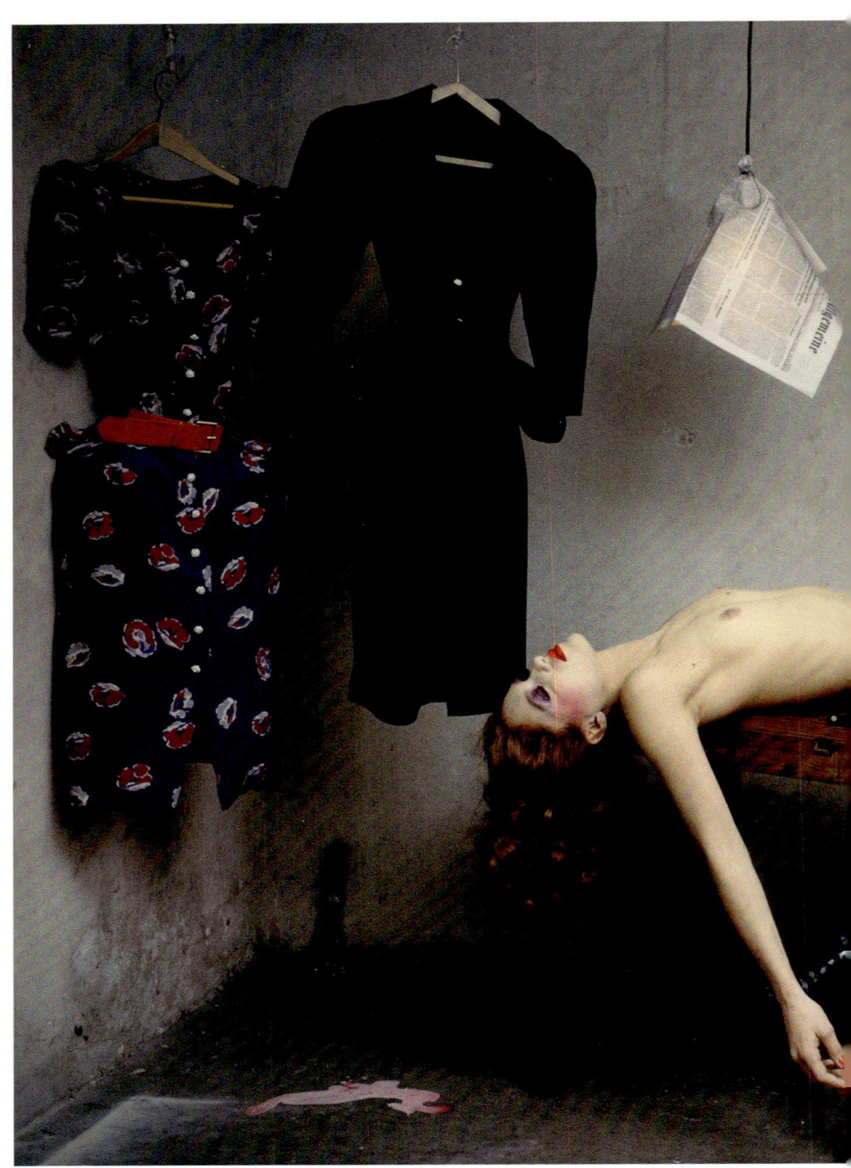

26. Unpublished, date unknown.

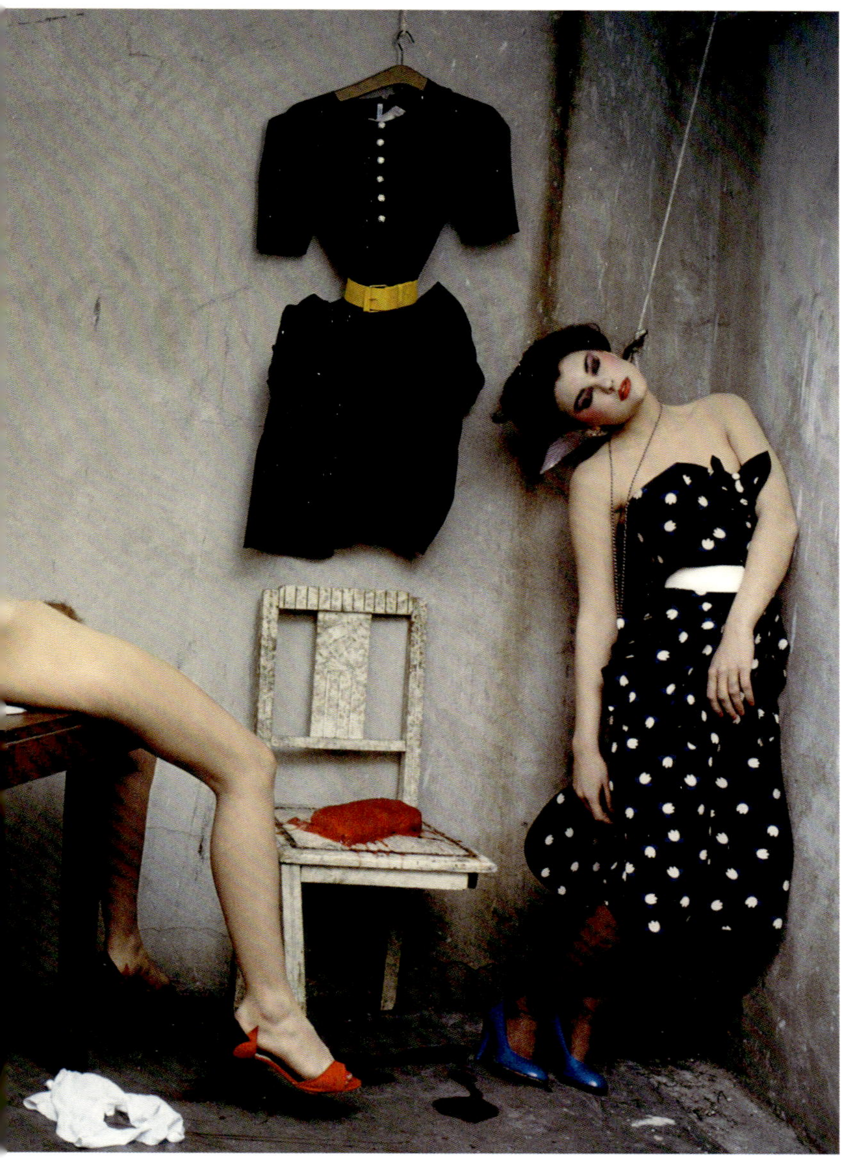

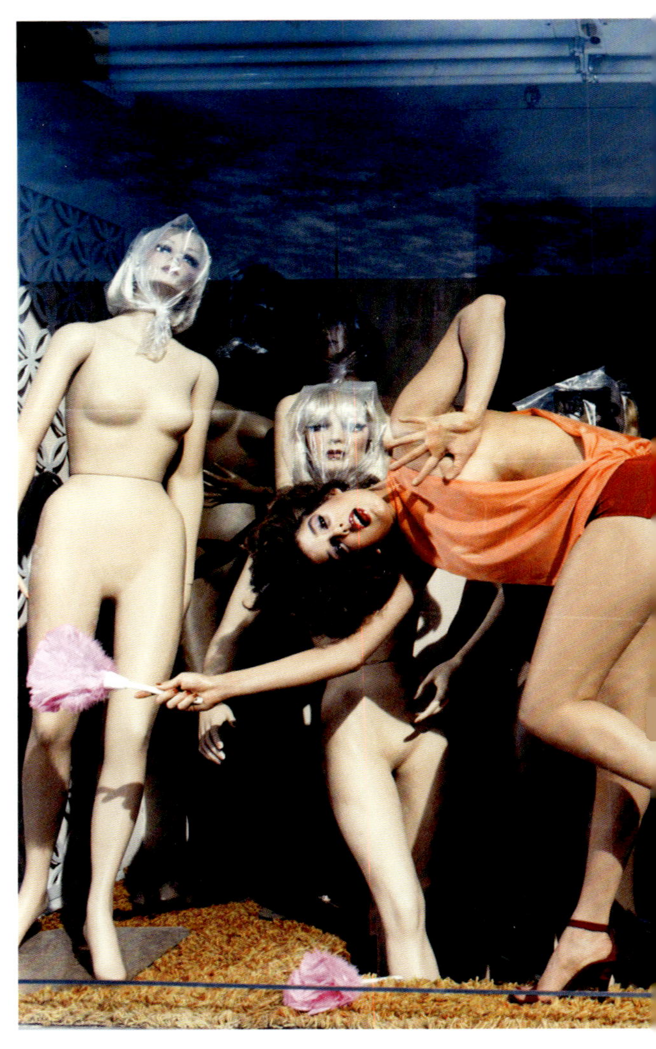

27. Campaign for Charles Jourdan, Spring 1978.

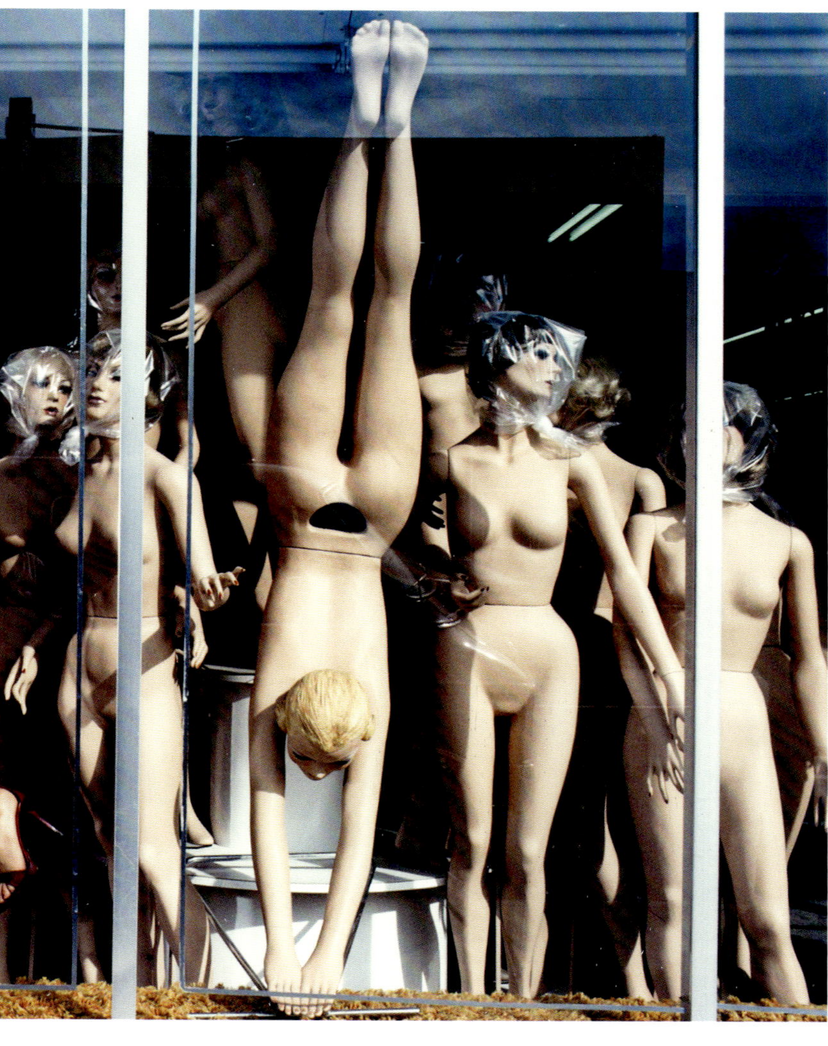

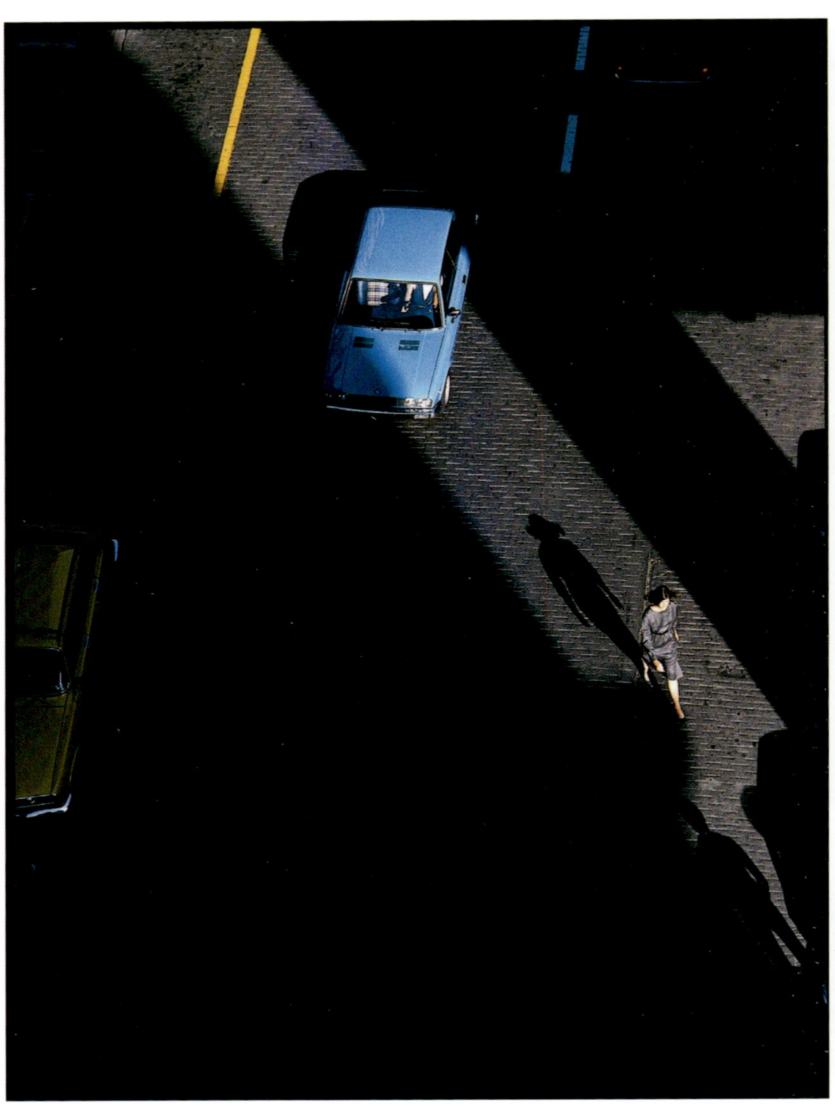

28. *Vogue France*, June 1975.

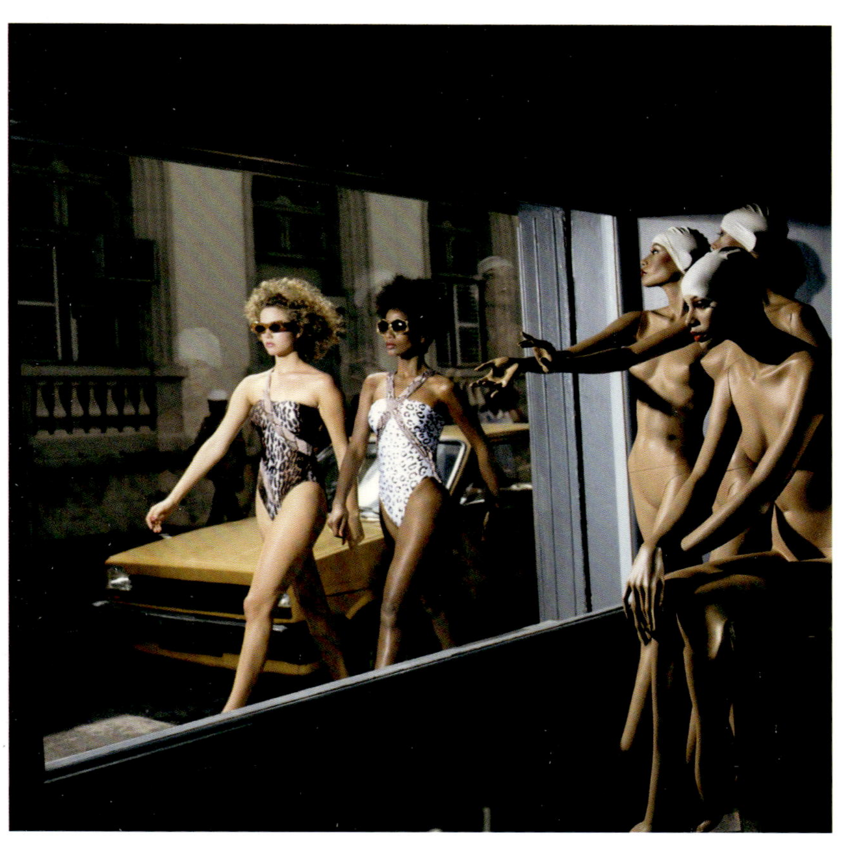

29. *Vogue France*, July 1985.

30. Campaign for Charles Jourdan, Spring 1978.

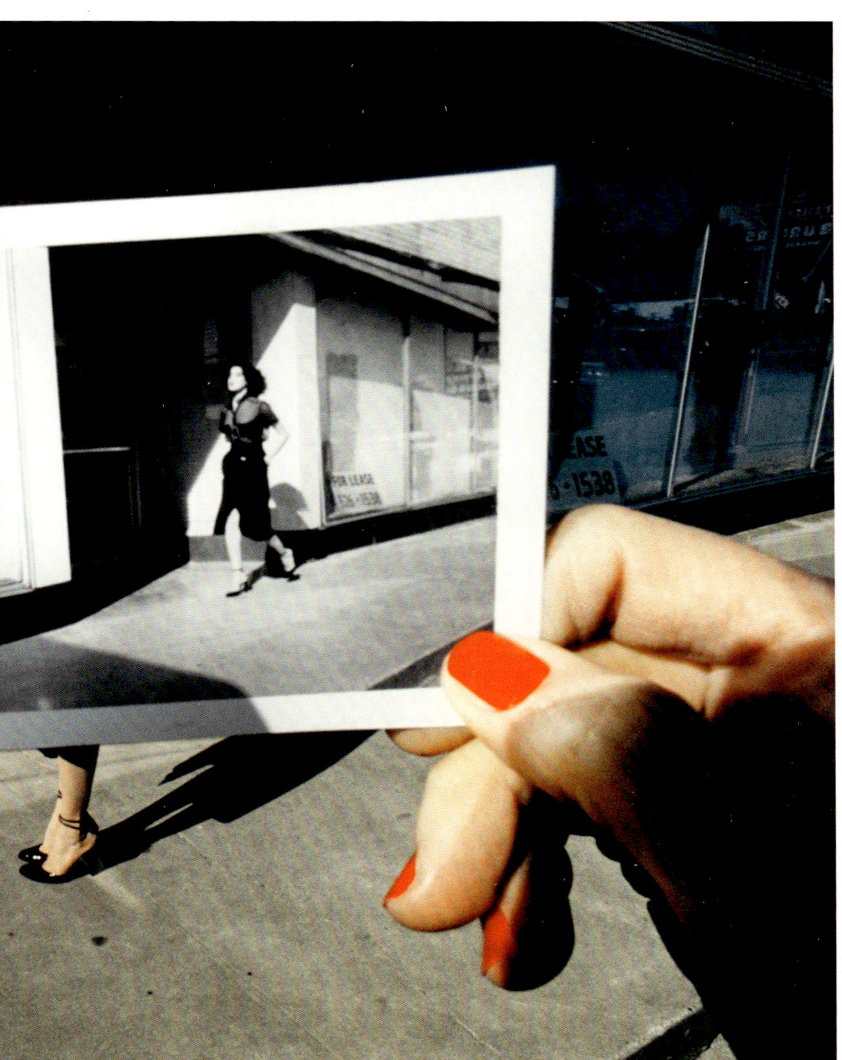

EASE
5 · 1538

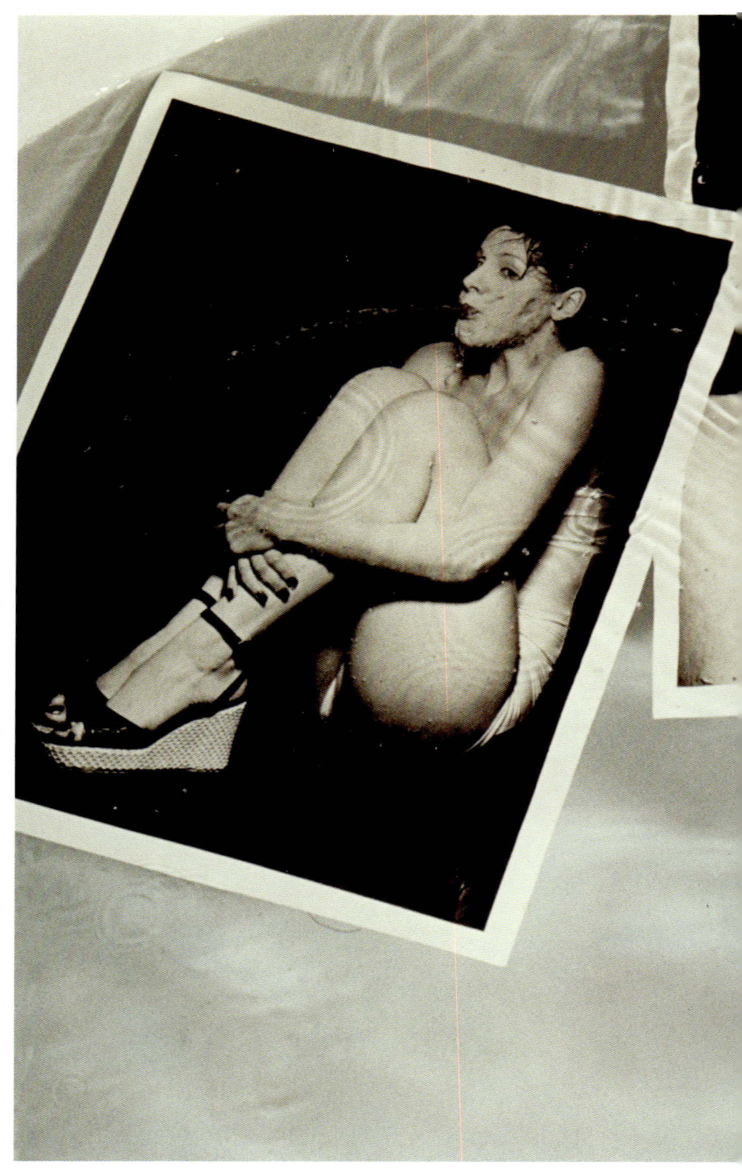

31. Campaign for Charles Jourdan, Summer 1975.

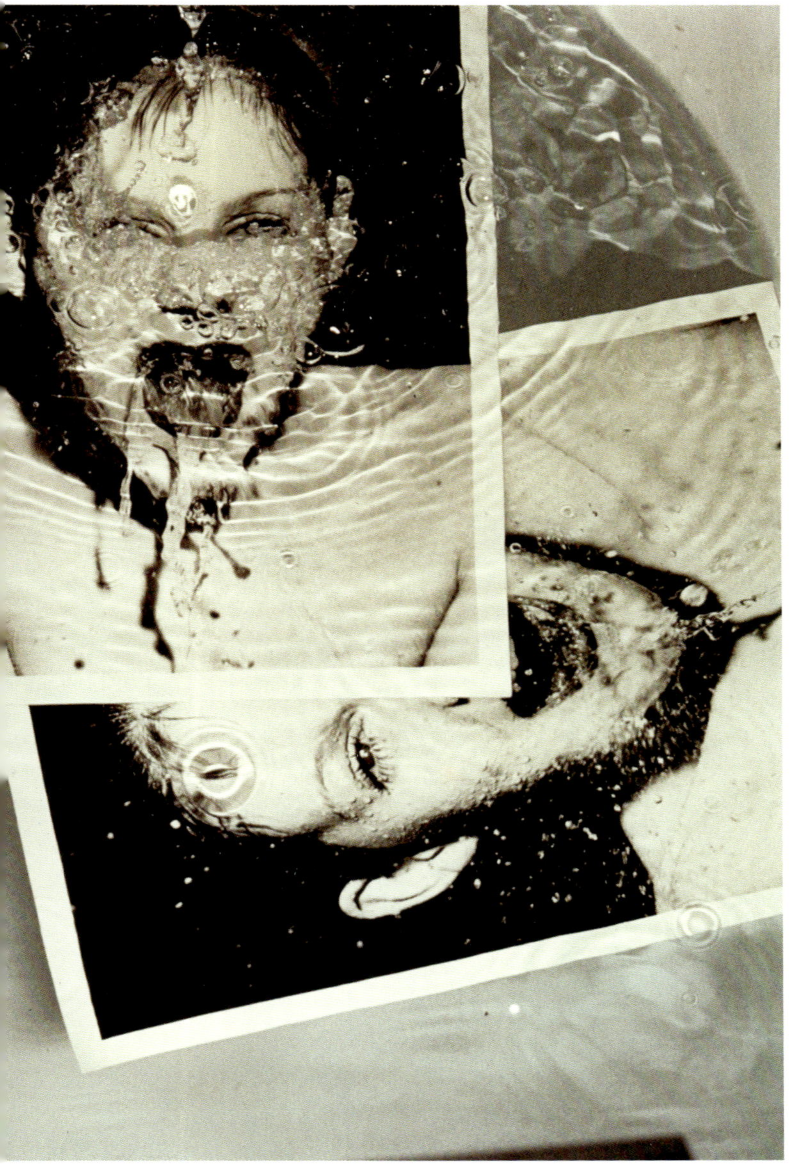

32. Campaign for Charles Jourdan, Spring 1978.

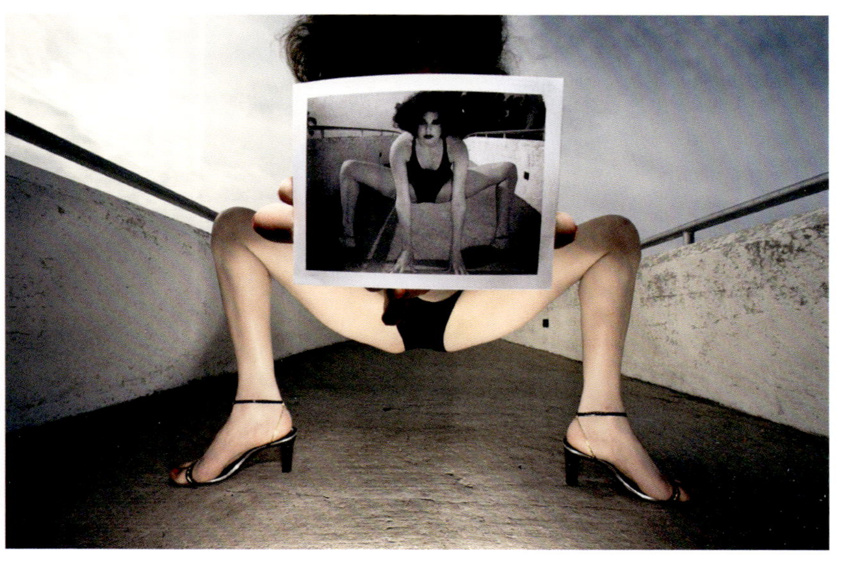

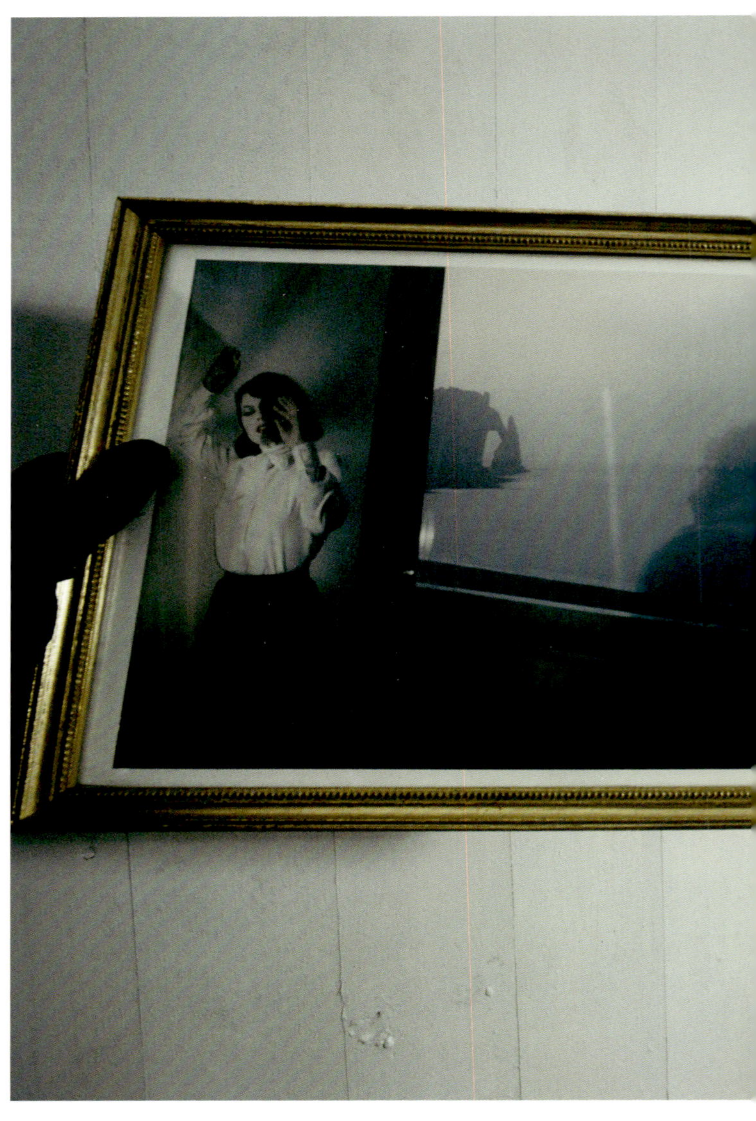

33. *Marie Claire France*, January 1980.

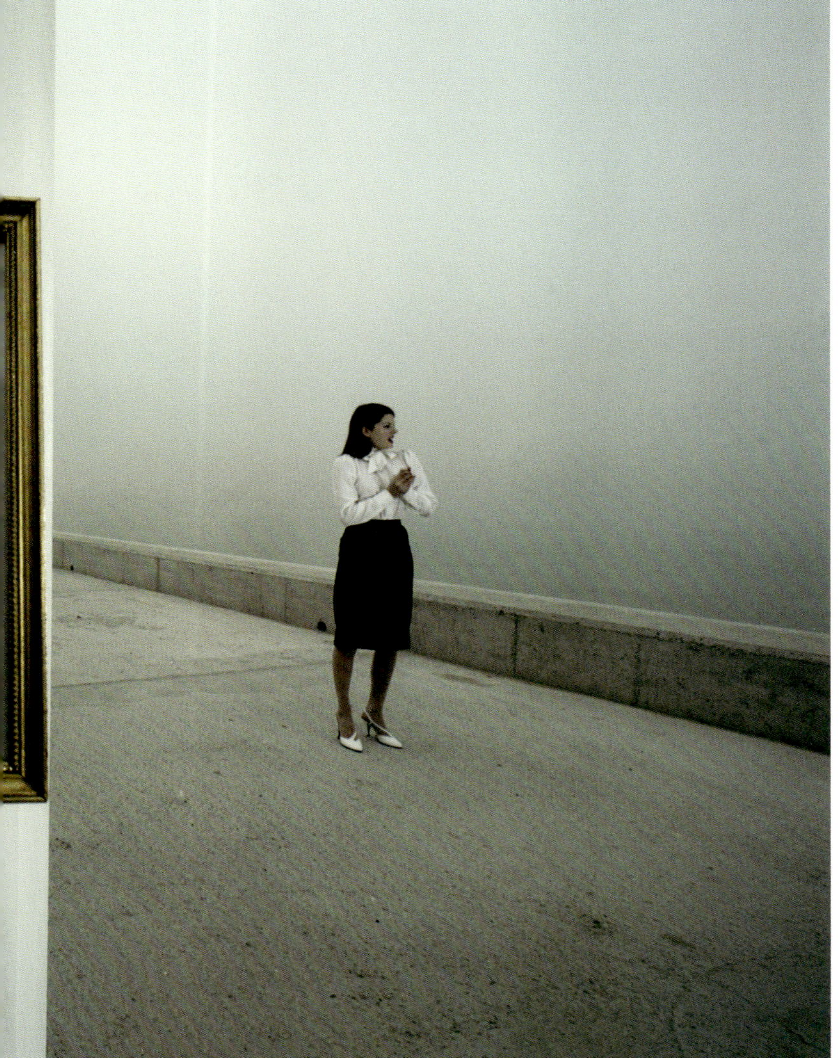

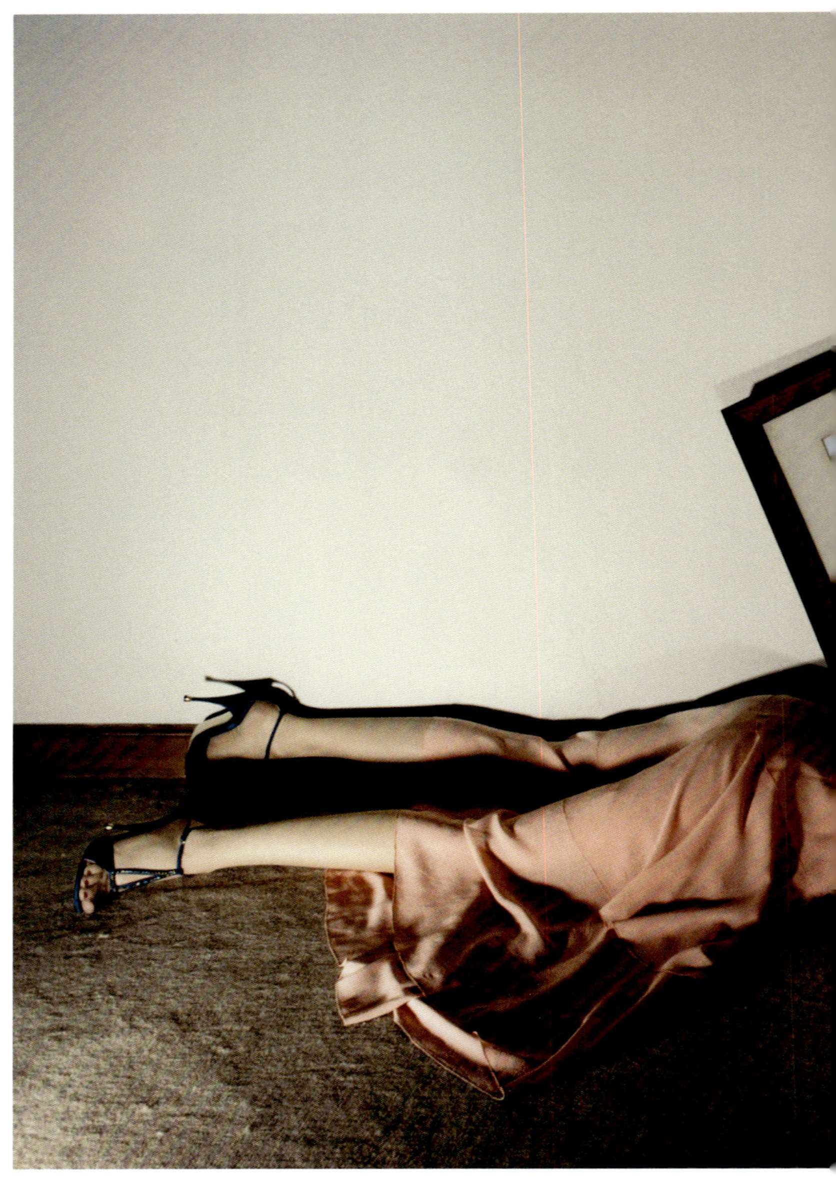

34. Guy Bourdin Archives, date unknown.

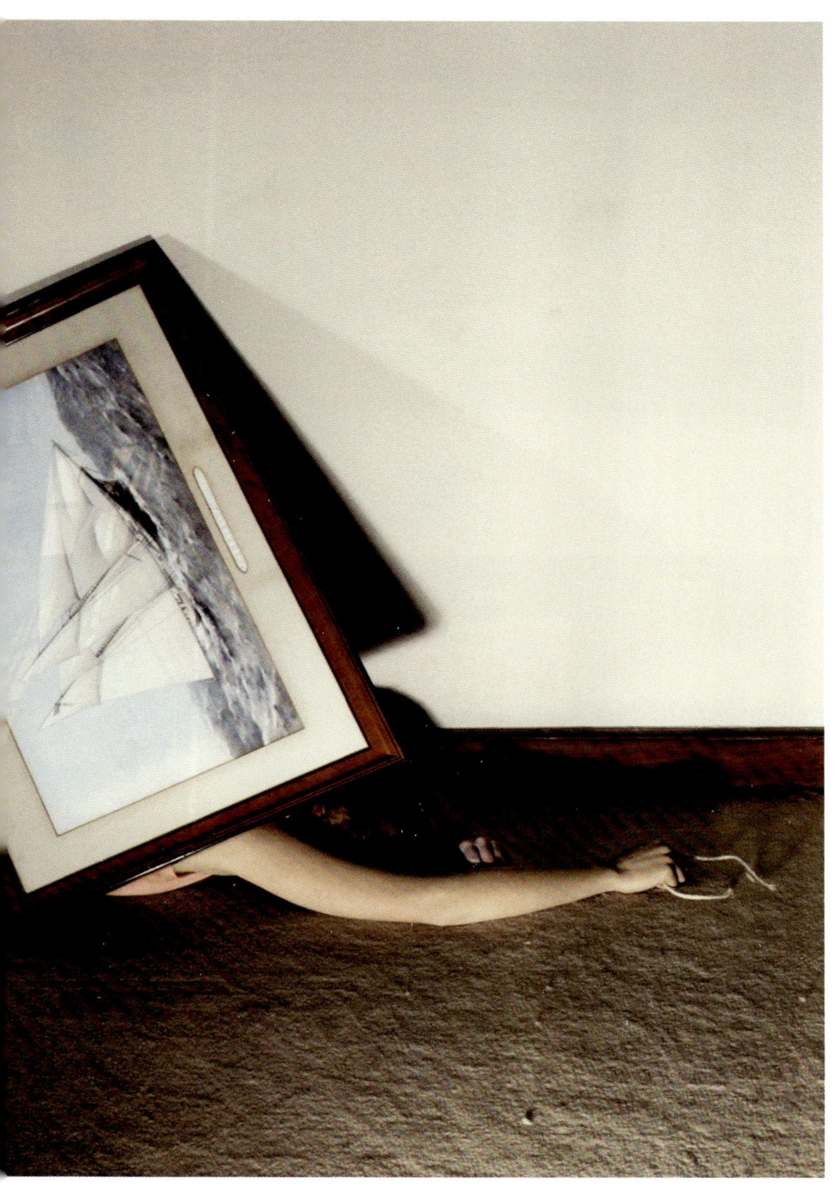

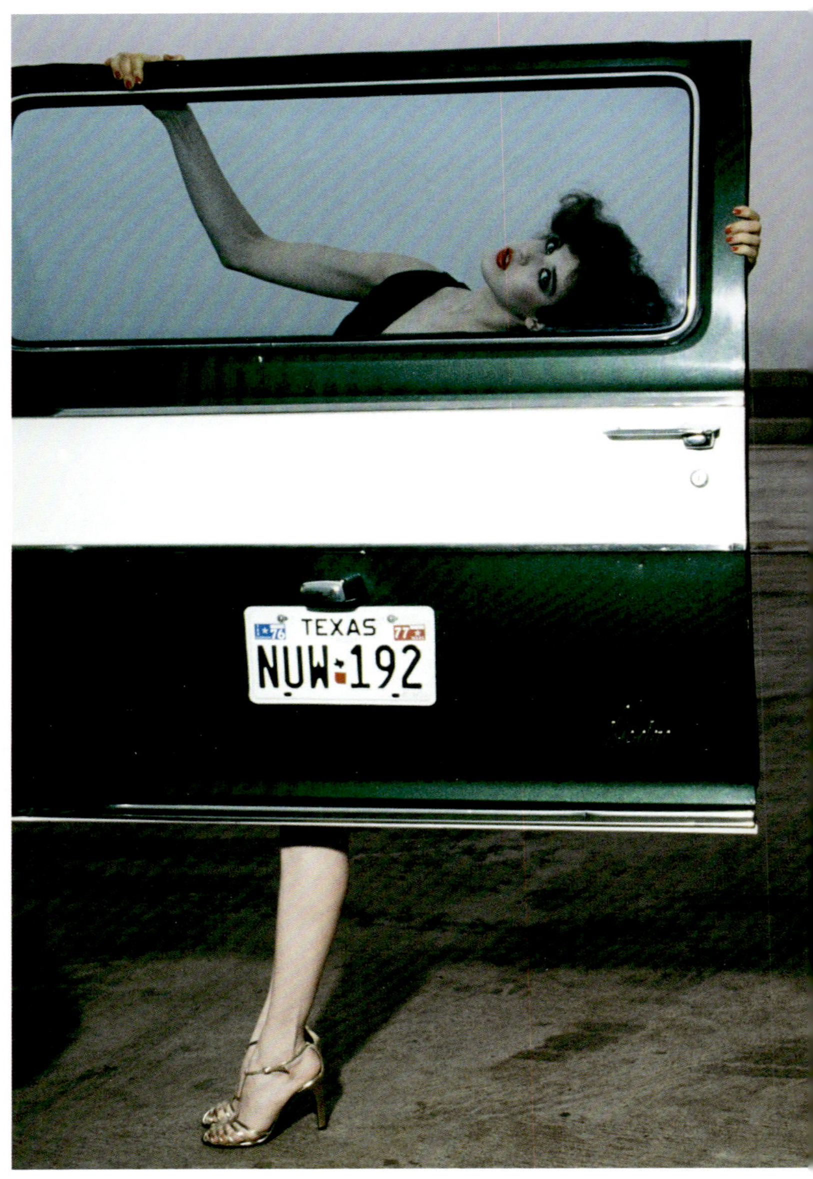

35. Campaign for Charles Jourdan, Summer 1978.

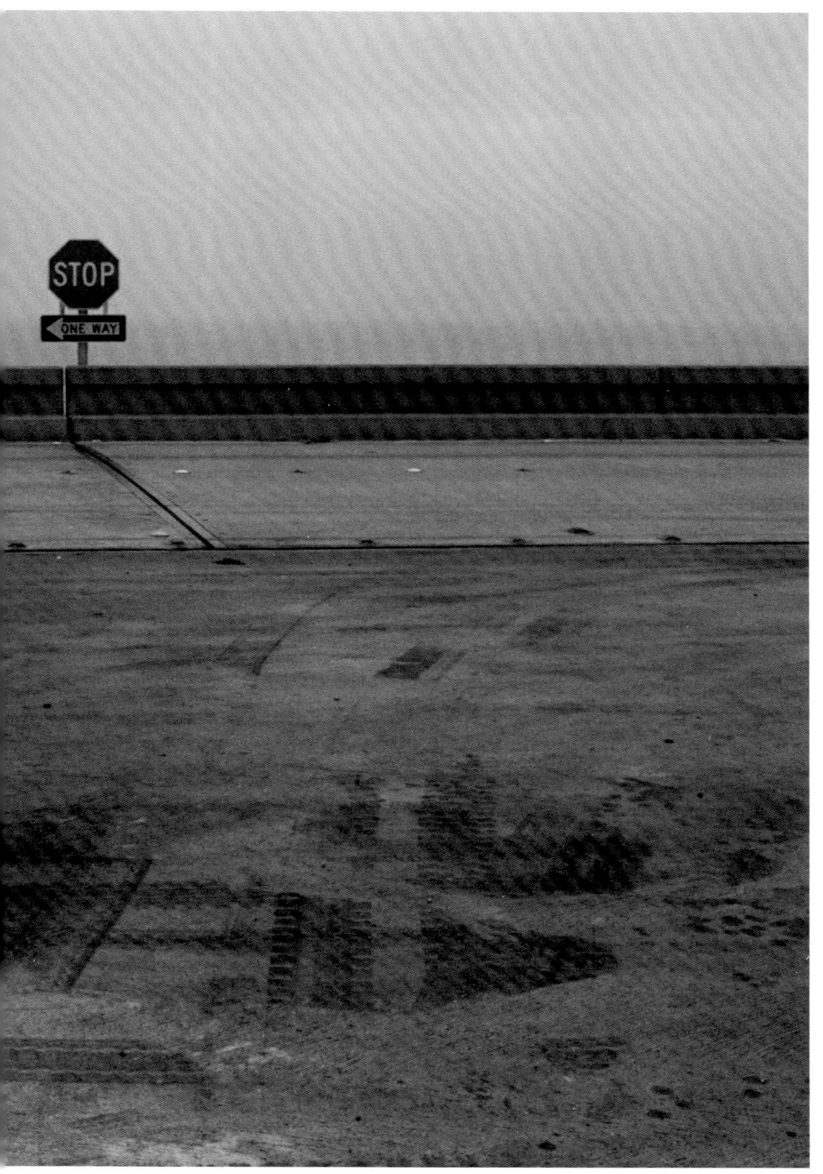
STOP
ONE WAY

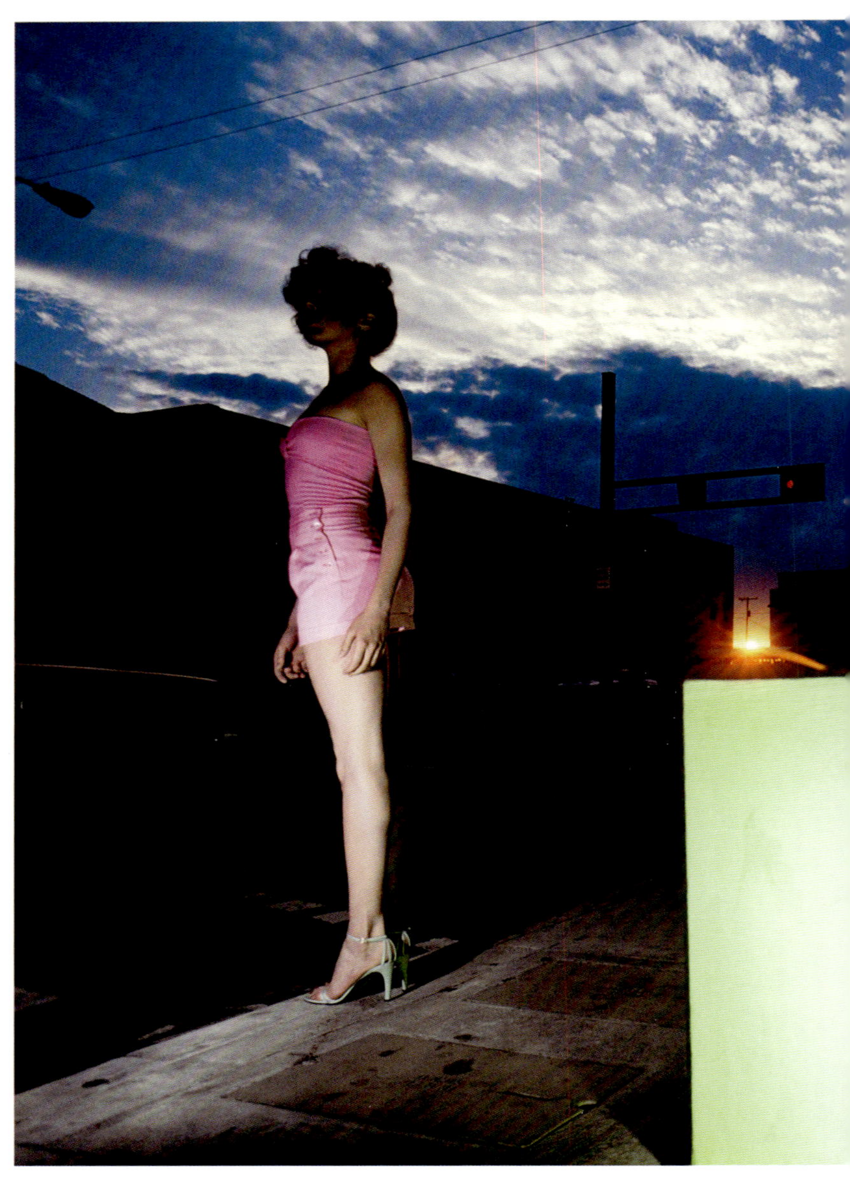

36. Campaign for Charles Jourdan, variant, Spring 1978.

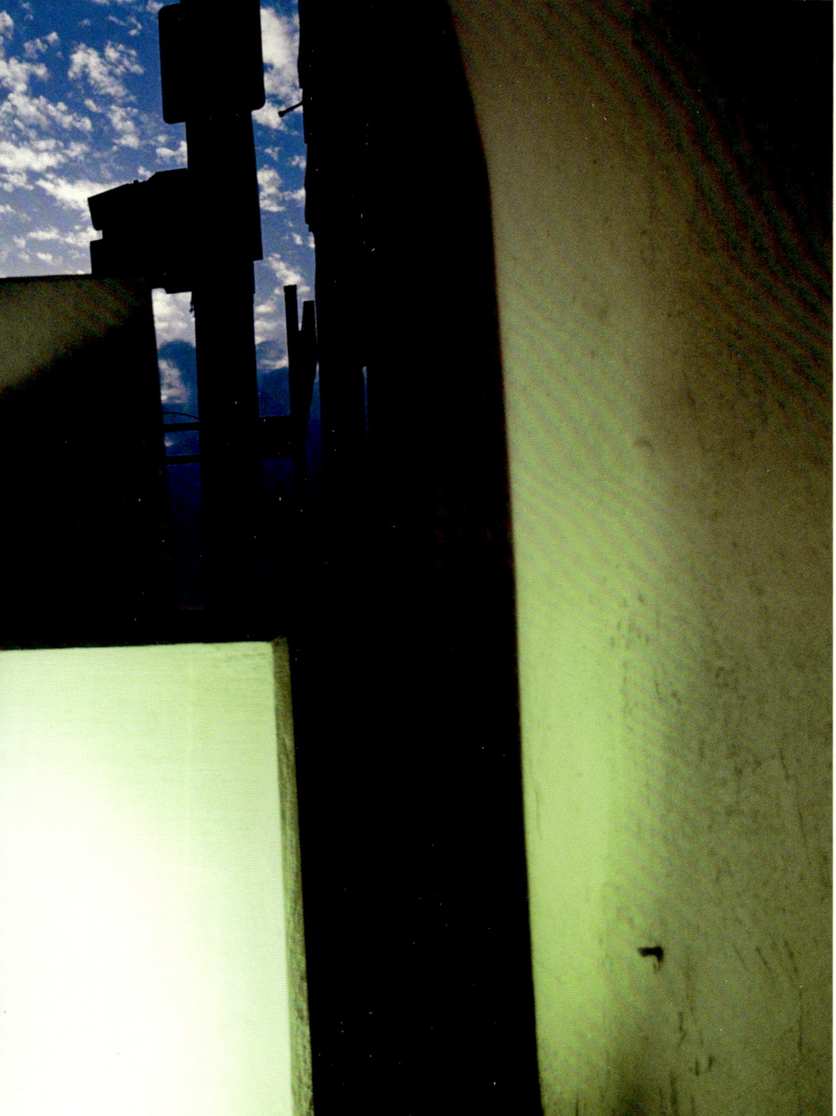

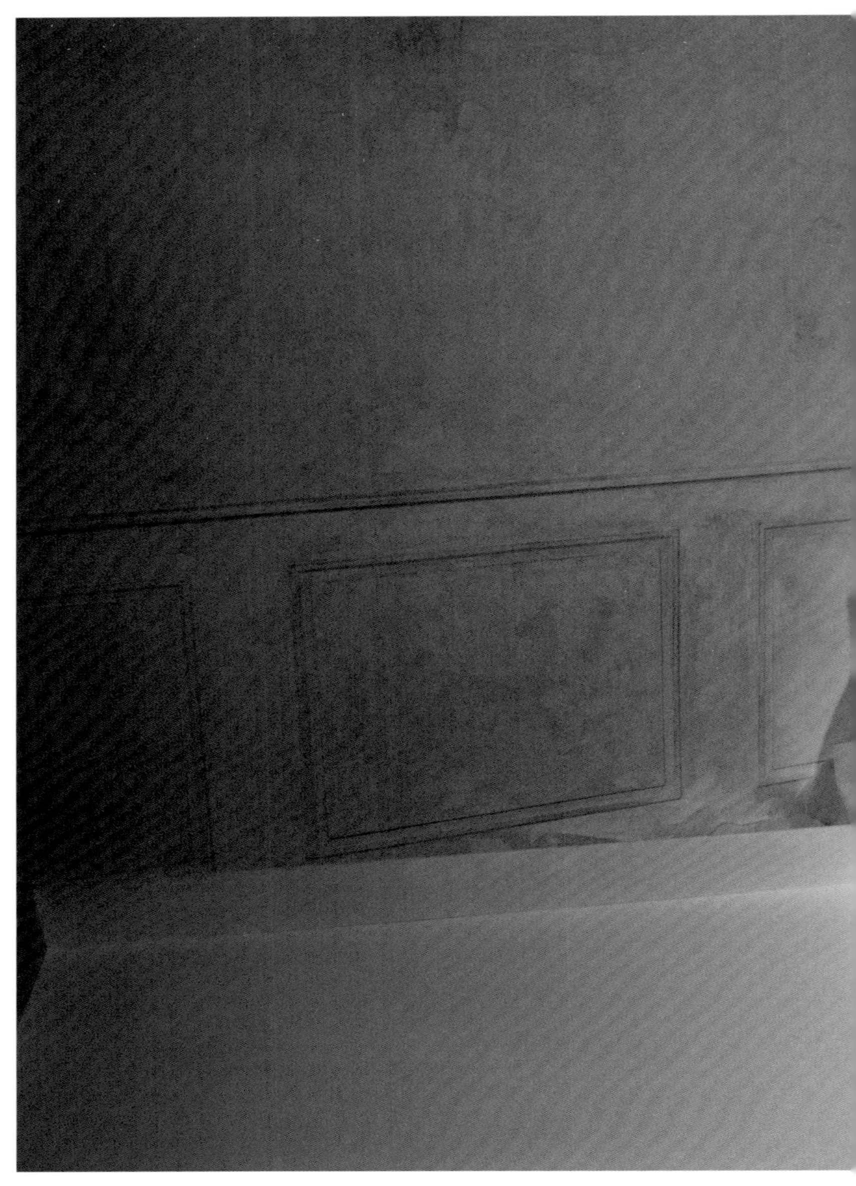

37. Campaign for Charles Jourdan, variant, Summer 1978.

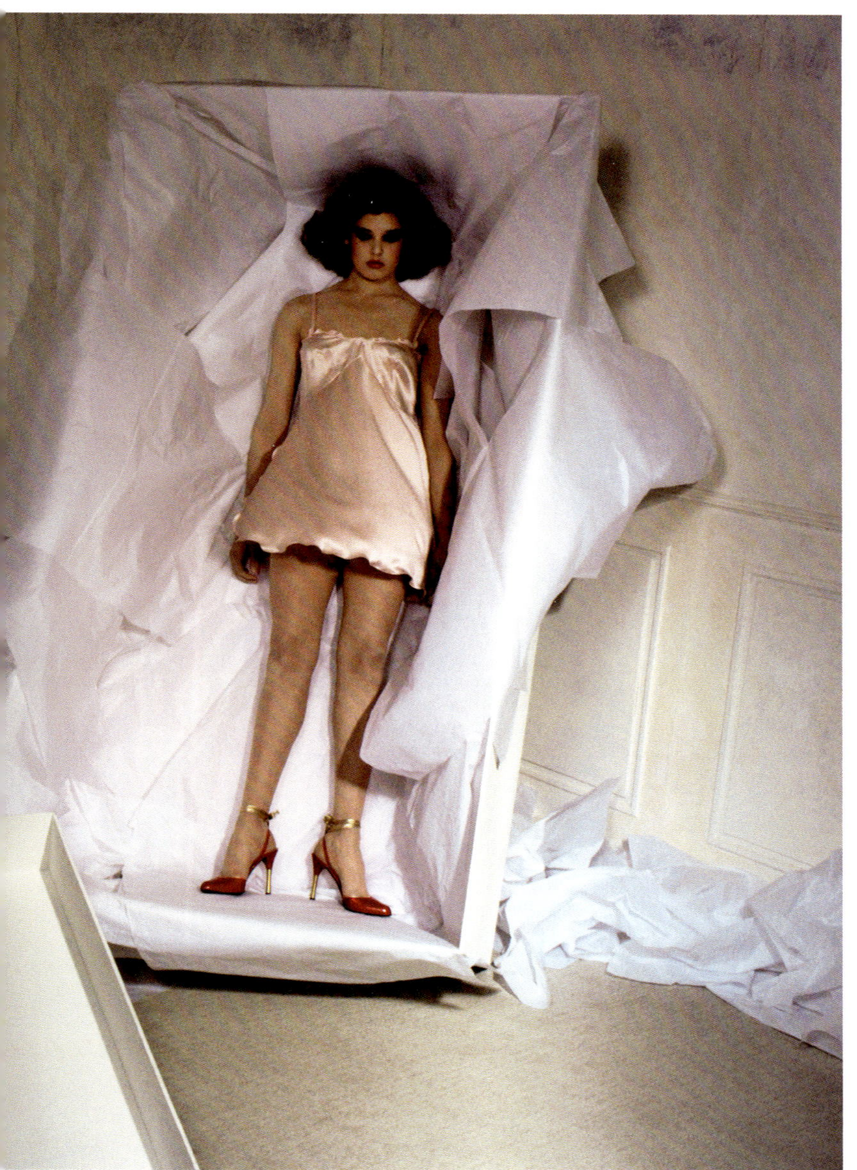

38. *Photo* magazine, September 1972.

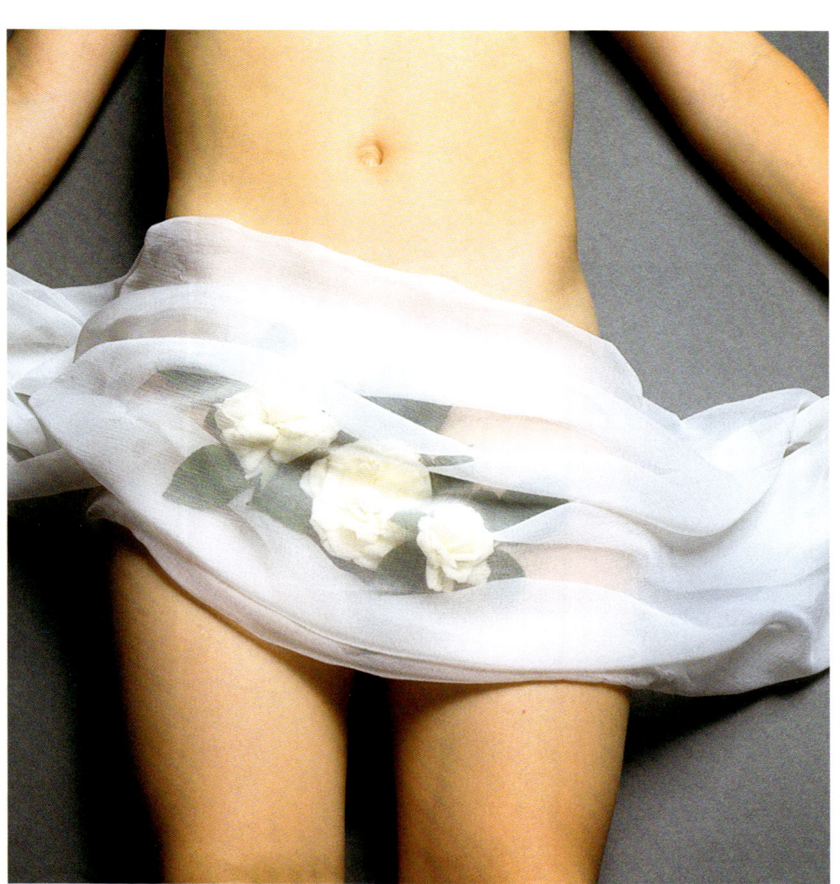

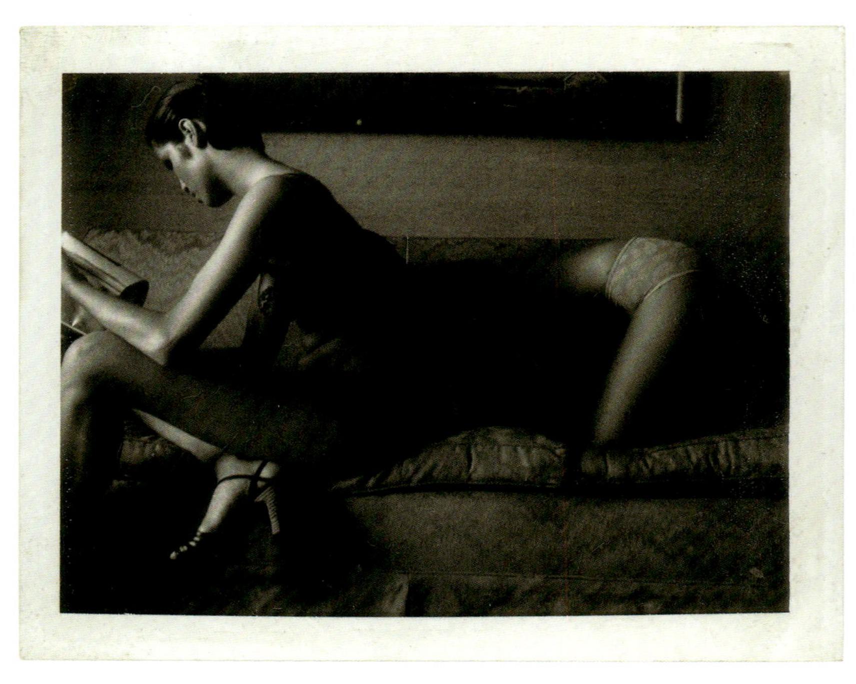

39. Guy Bourdin Archives, c. 1978.

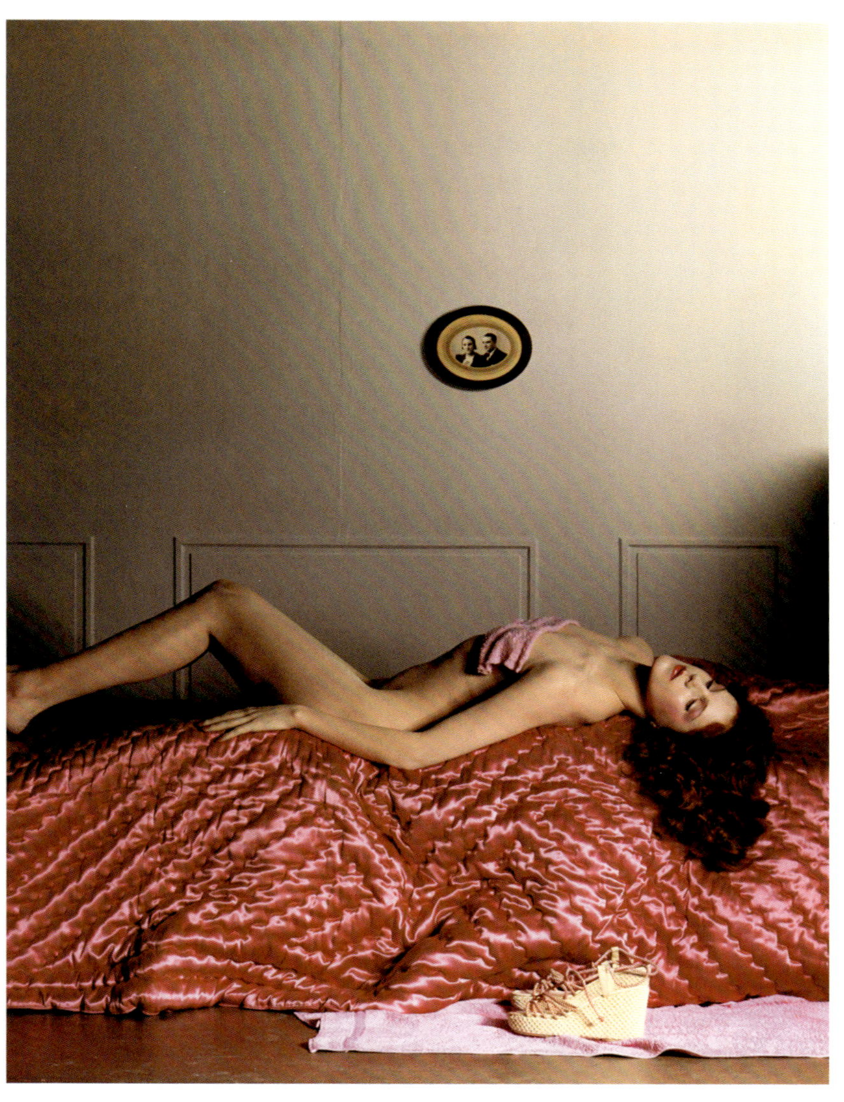

40. Campaign for Charles Jourdan, Summer 1975.

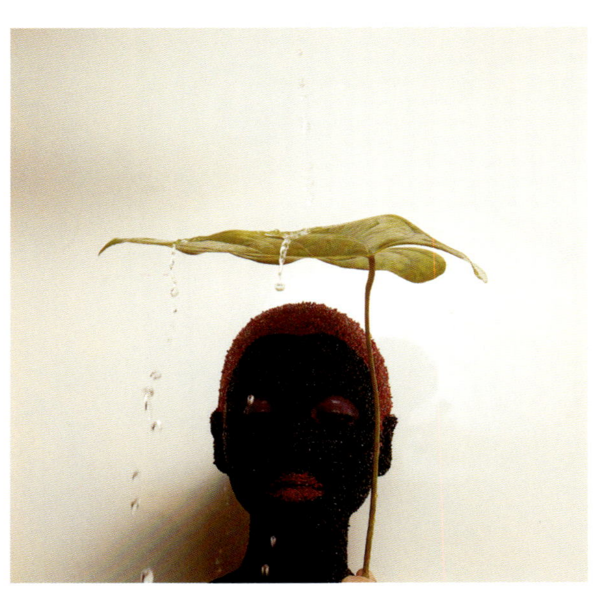

41. *Vogue France*, December 1969–January 1970.

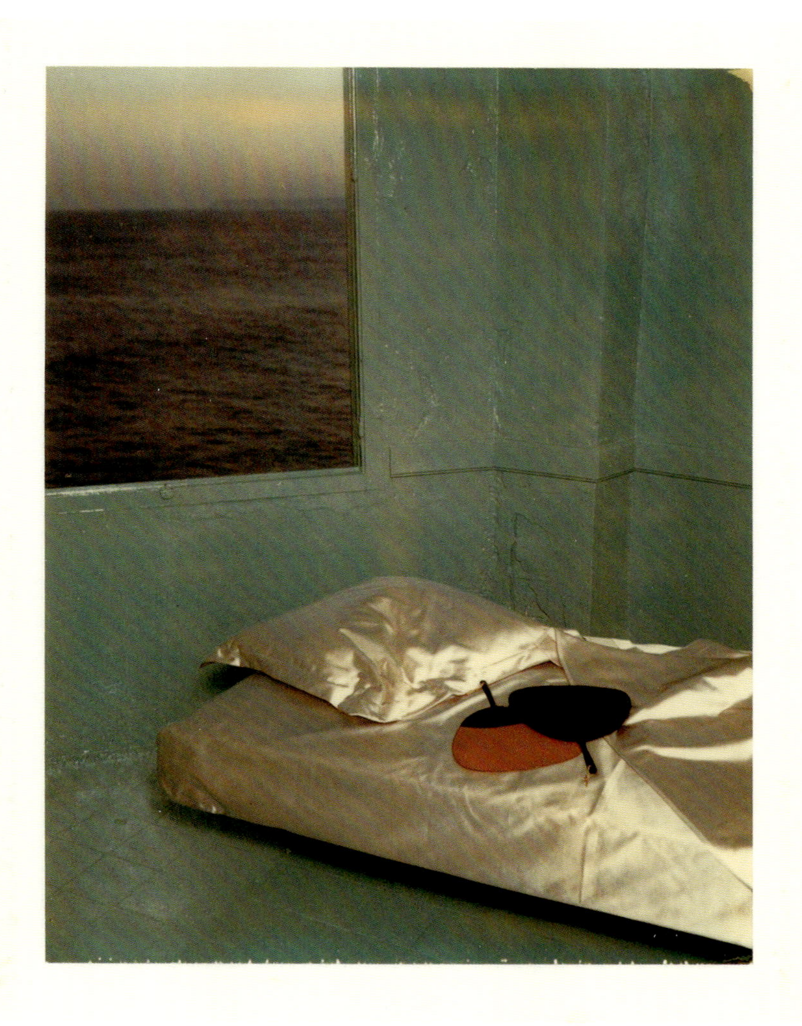

42. Guy Bourdin Archives, date unknown.

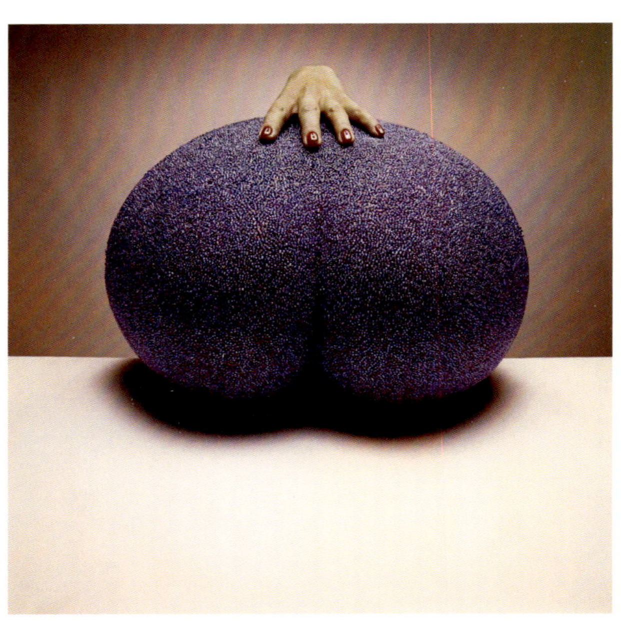

43. *Vogue France*, March 1971.

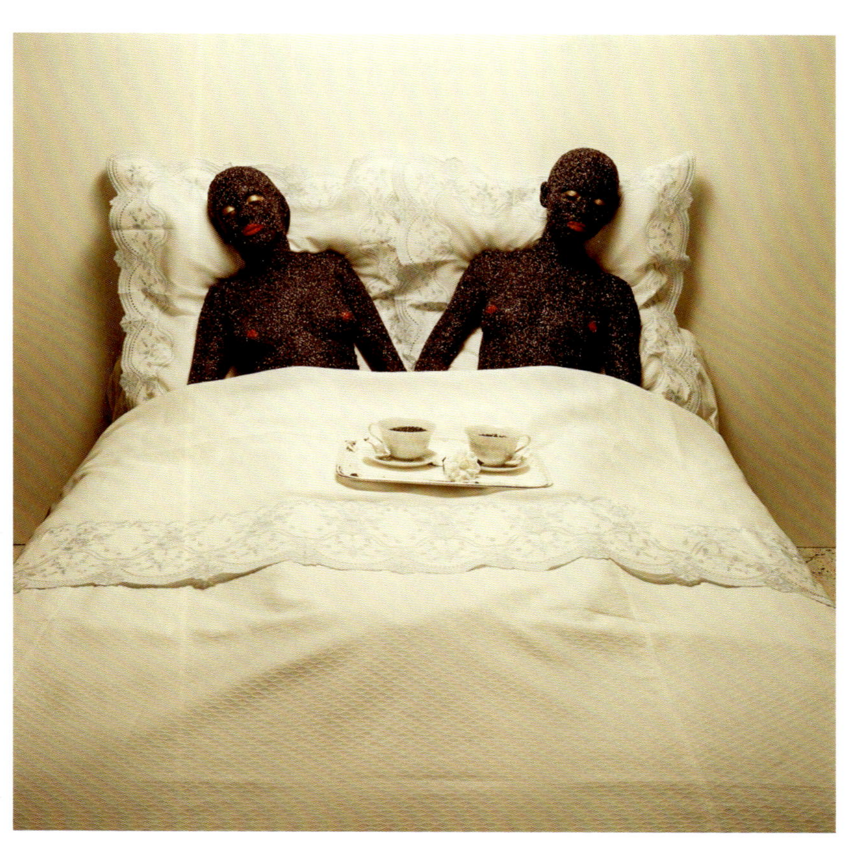

44. *Vogue France*, December 1969.

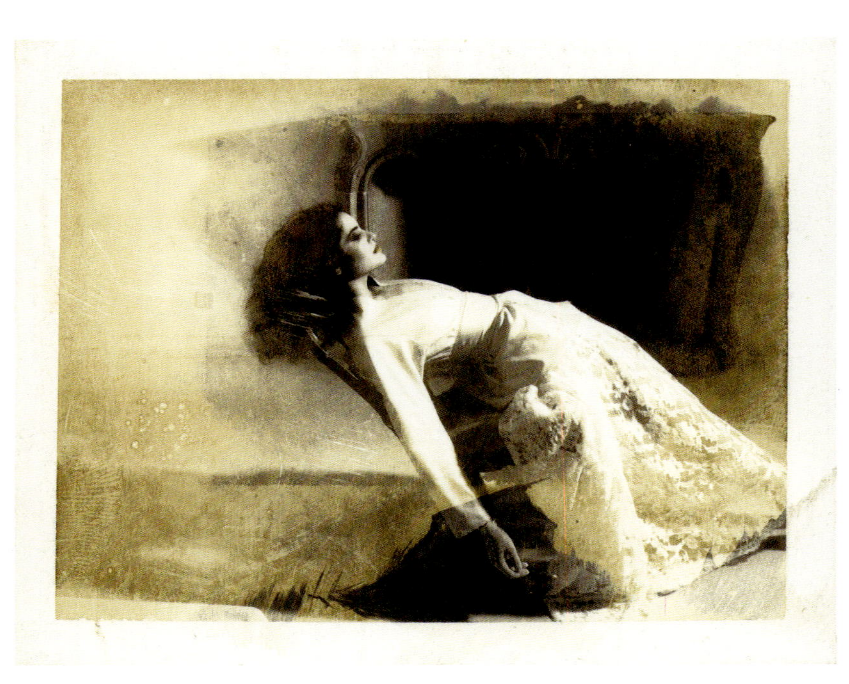

45. Guy Bourdin Archives, Summer 1978.

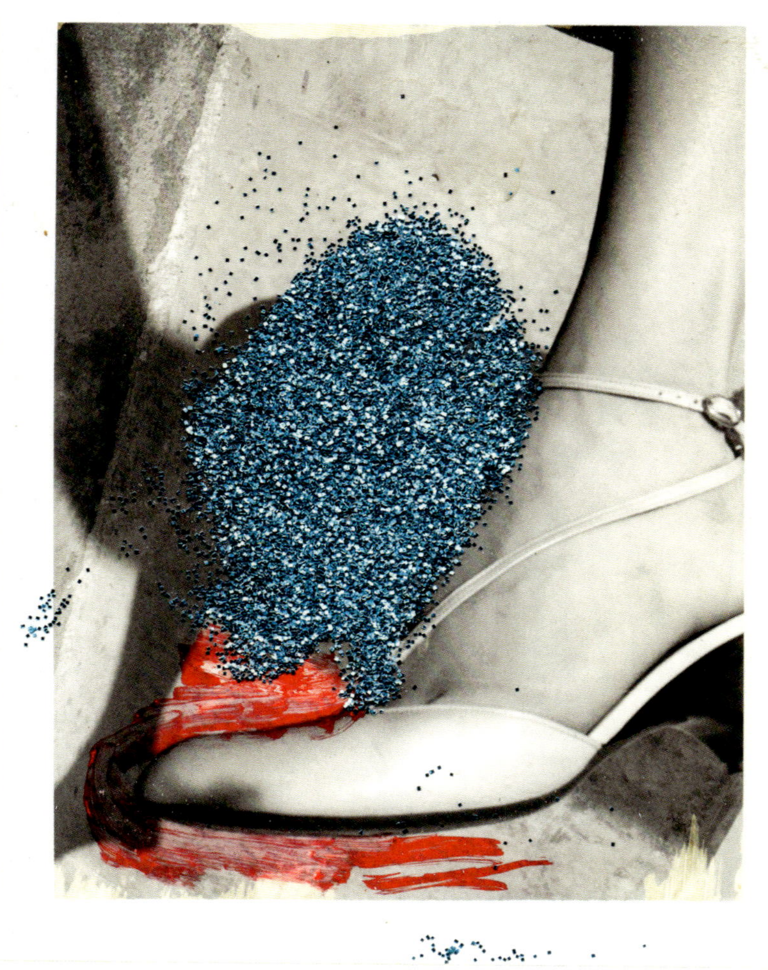

46. Guy Bourdin Archives, December 1977.

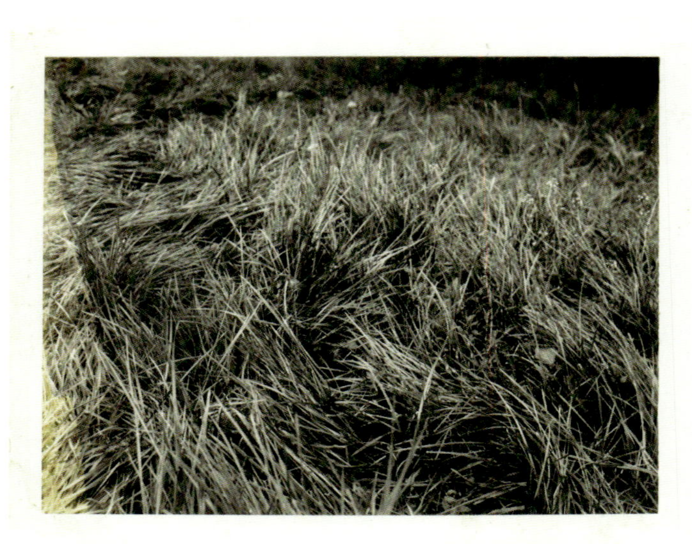

47. Guy Bourdin Archives, date unknown.

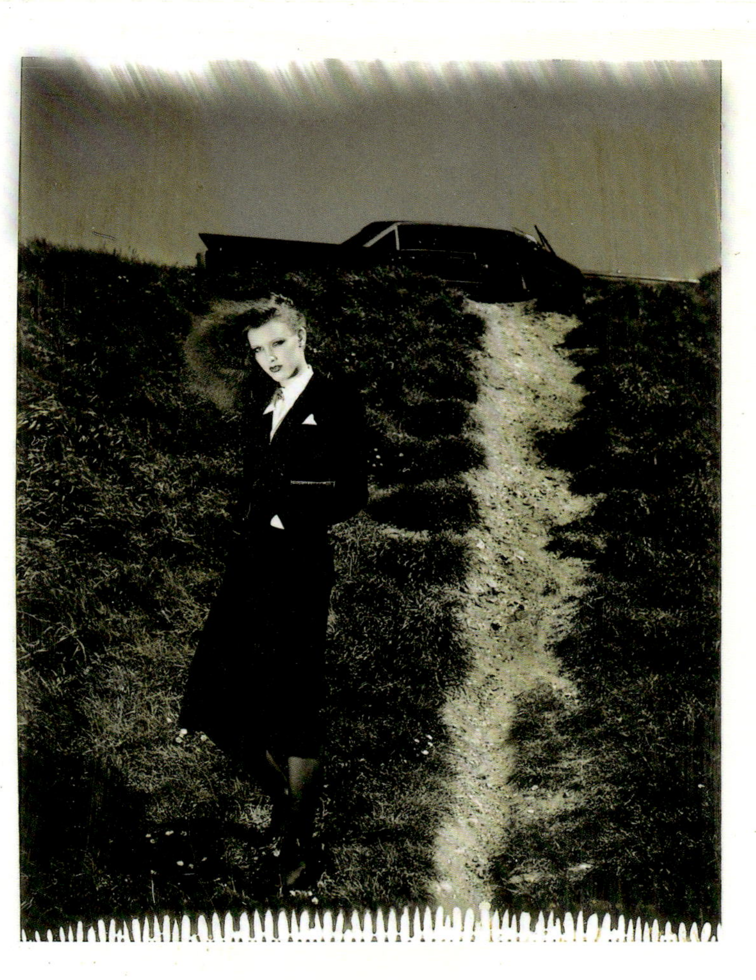

48. Guy Bourdin Archives, c. 1975.

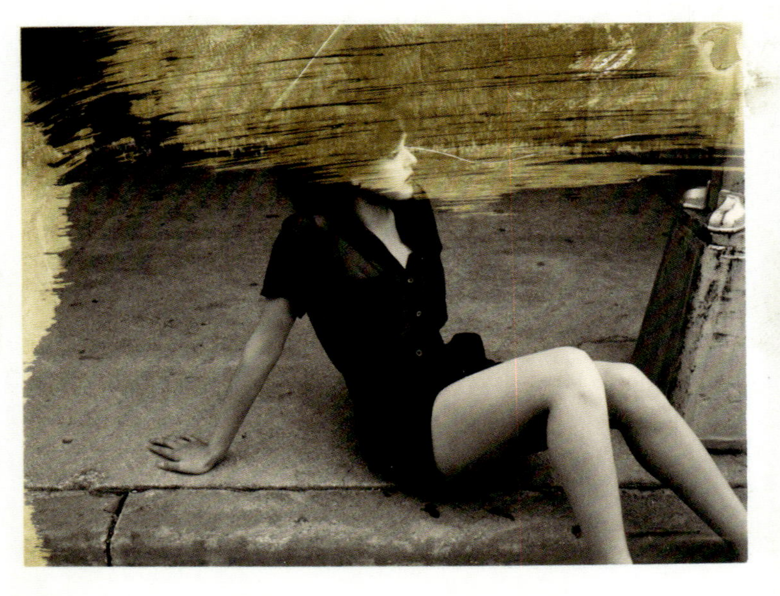

49. Guy Bourdin Archives, January 1978.

Opposite:
50. Guy Bourdin Archives, variant, September 1972.

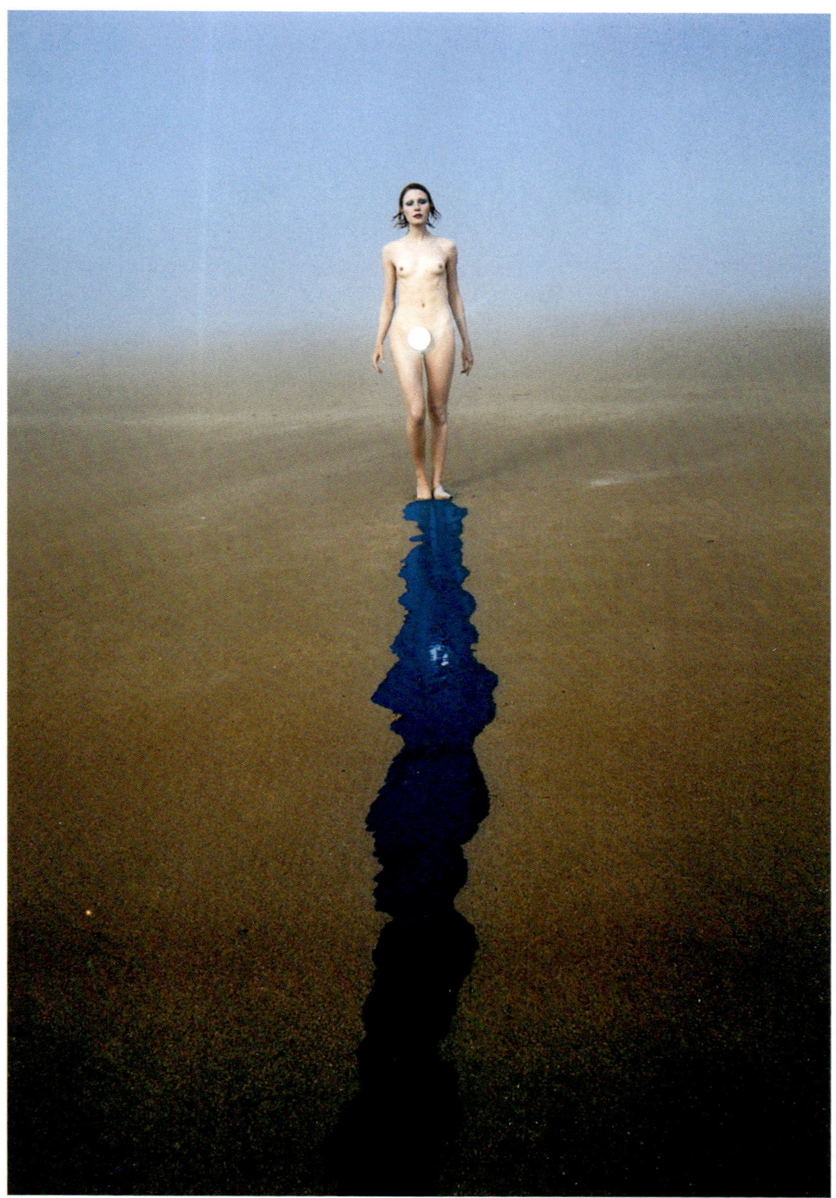

51. Walking legs, date unknown.

Overleaf:
52. Guy Bourdin Archives, January 1978.

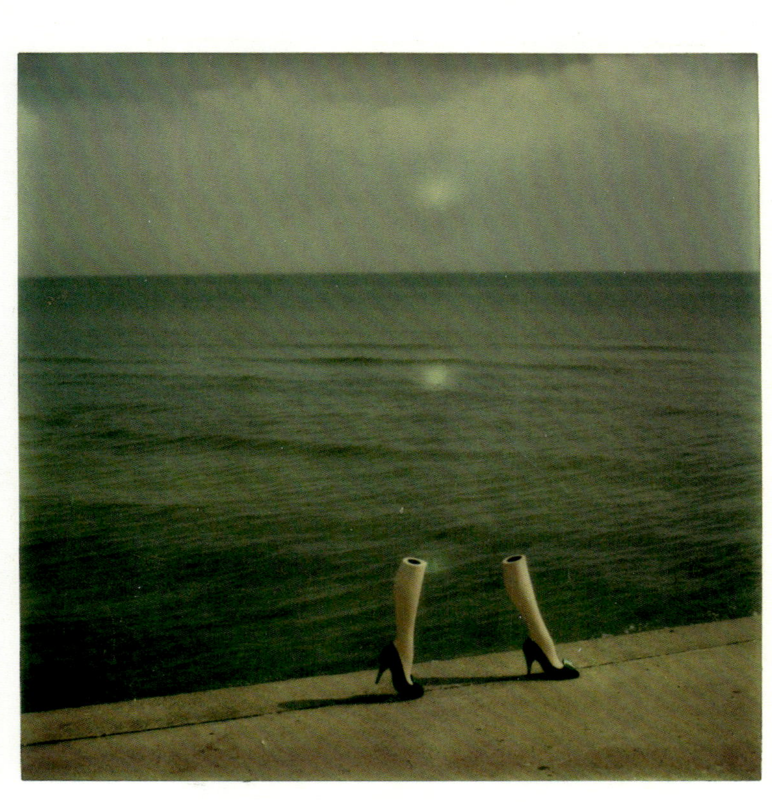

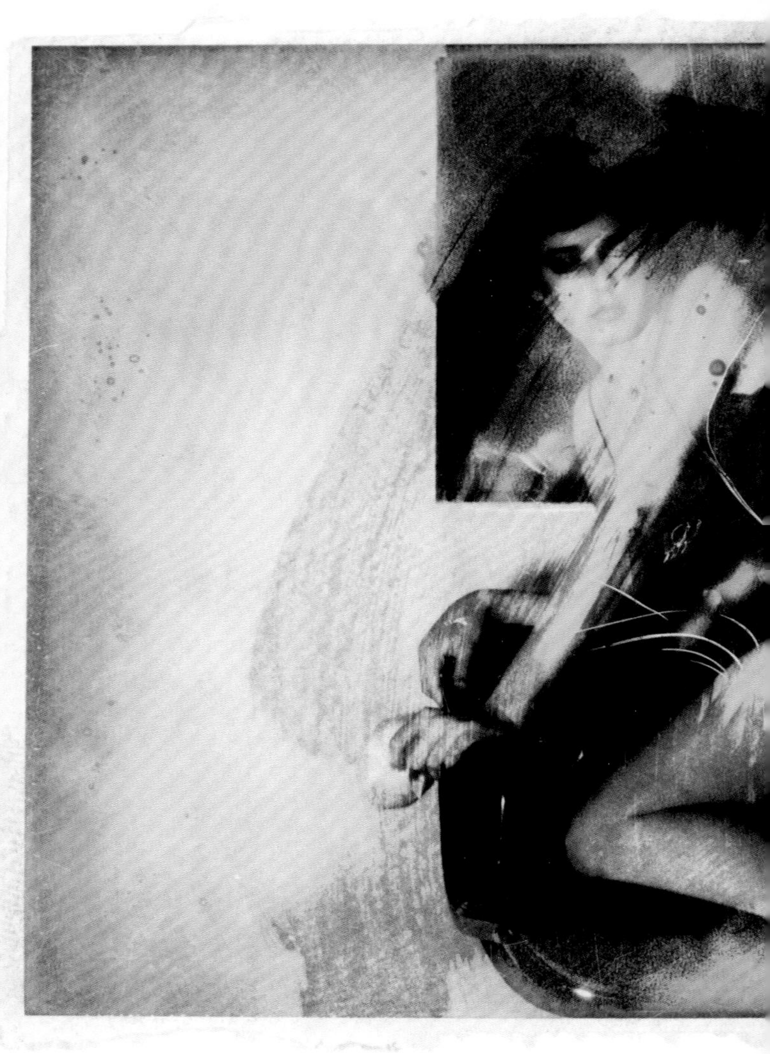

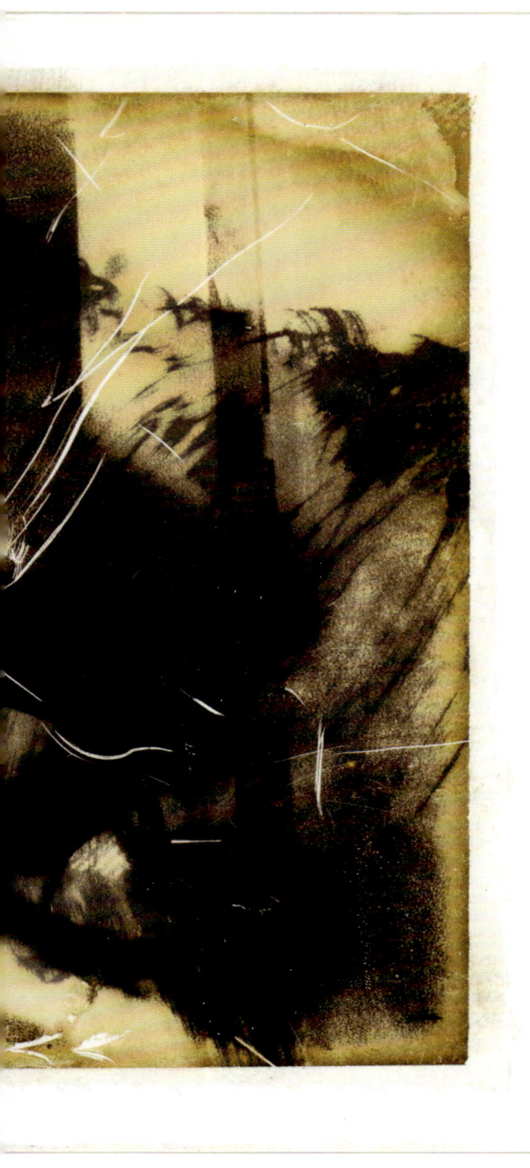

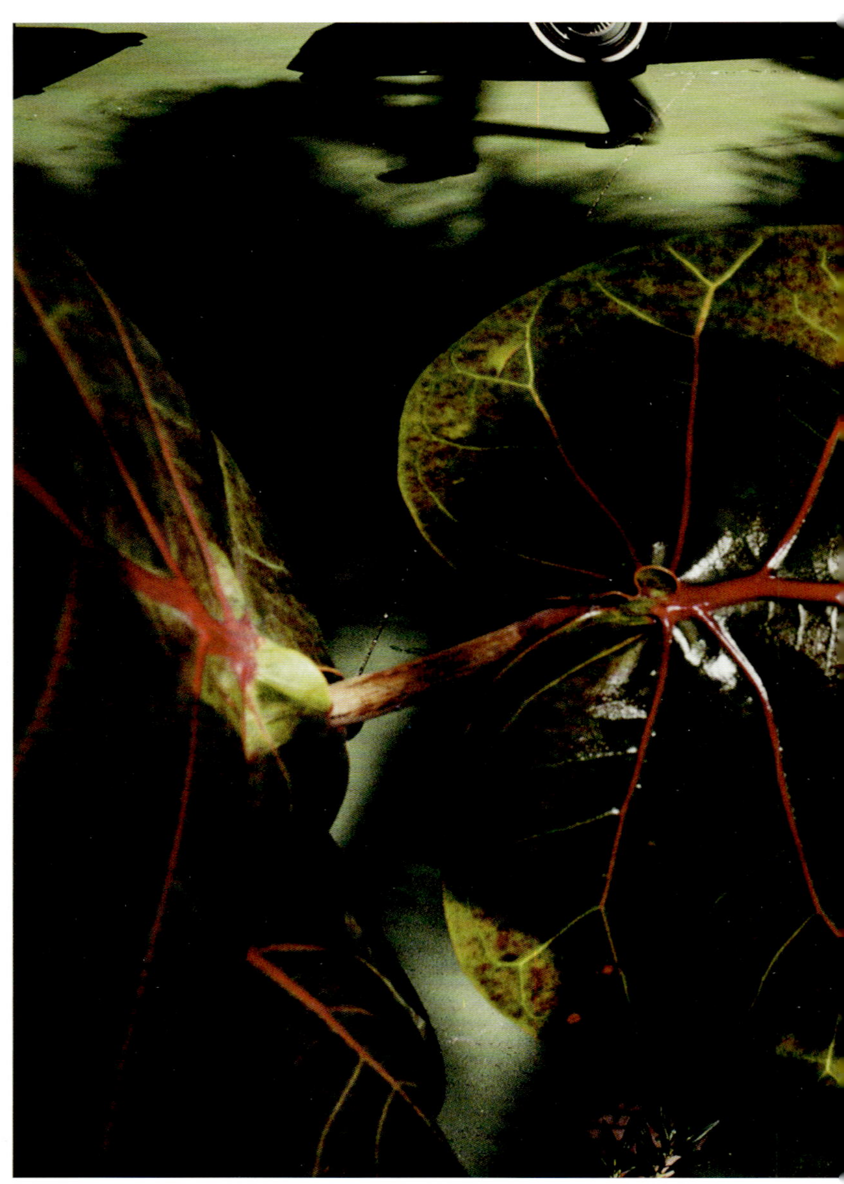

53. Campaign for Charles Jourdan, Summer 1978.

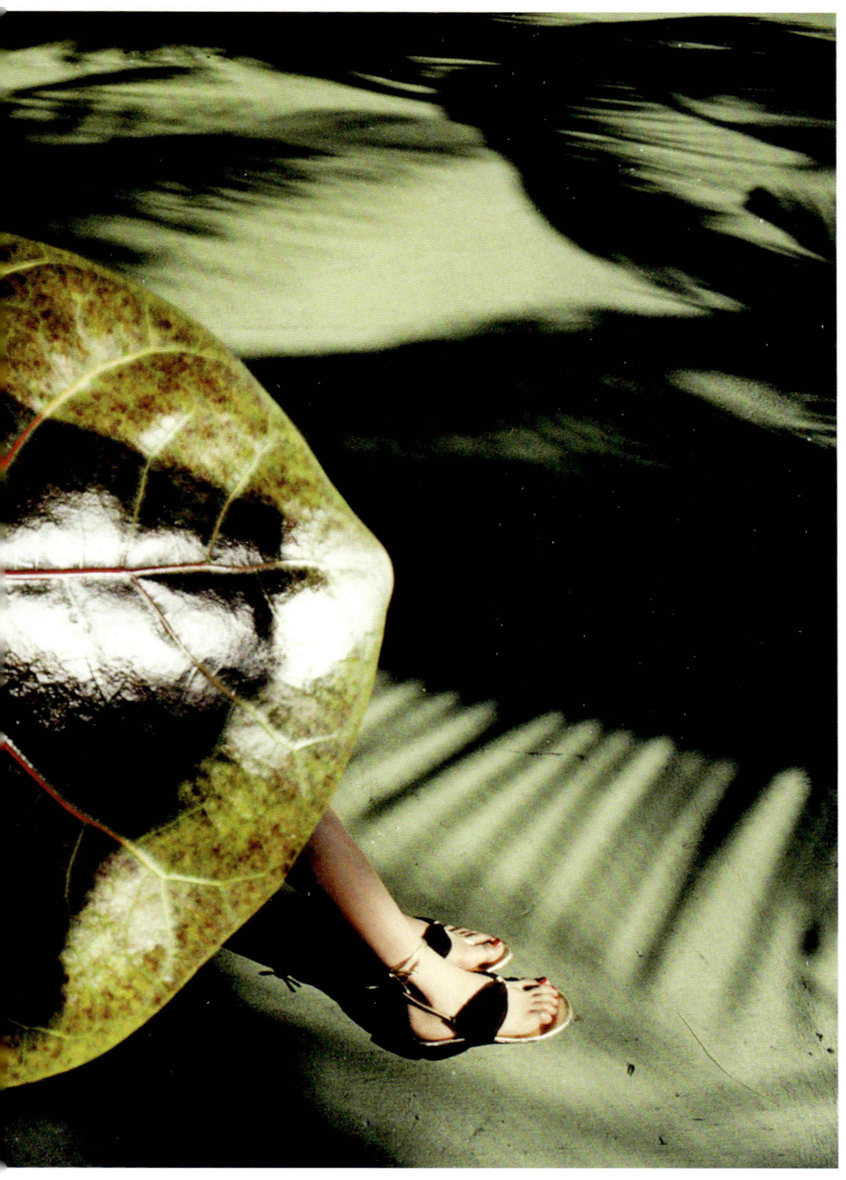

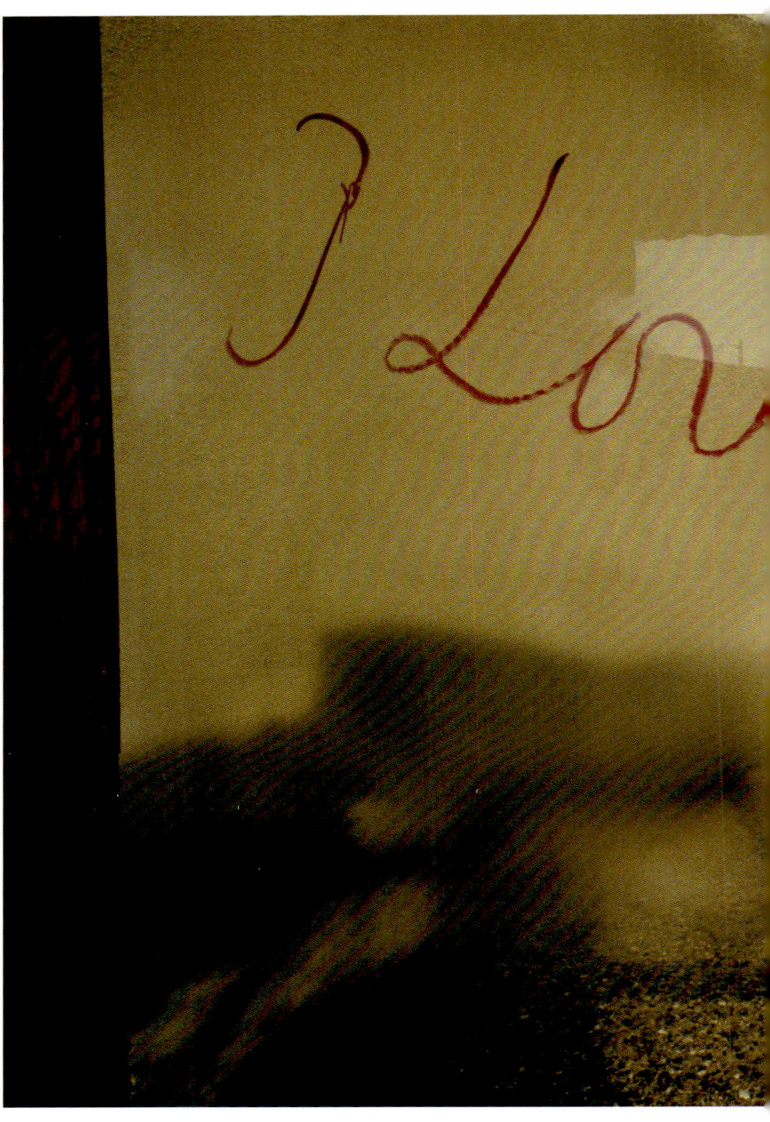

54. Guy Bourdin Archives, date unknown.

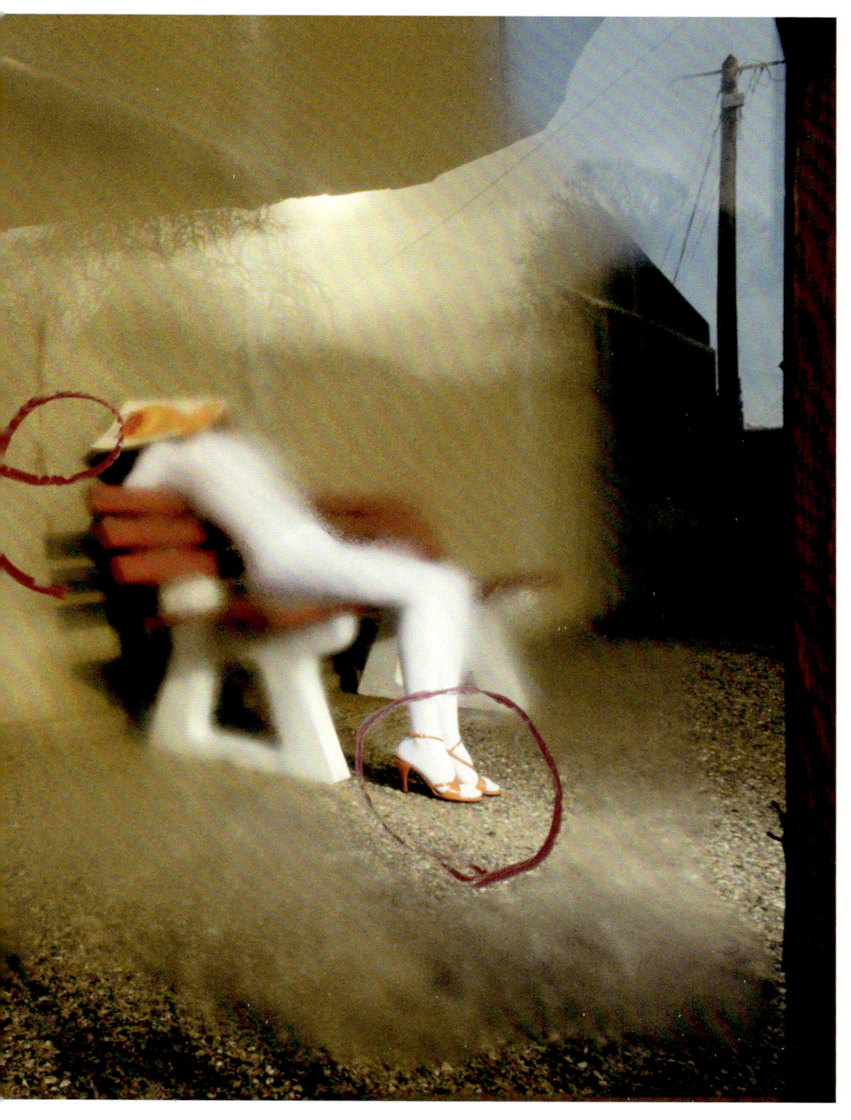

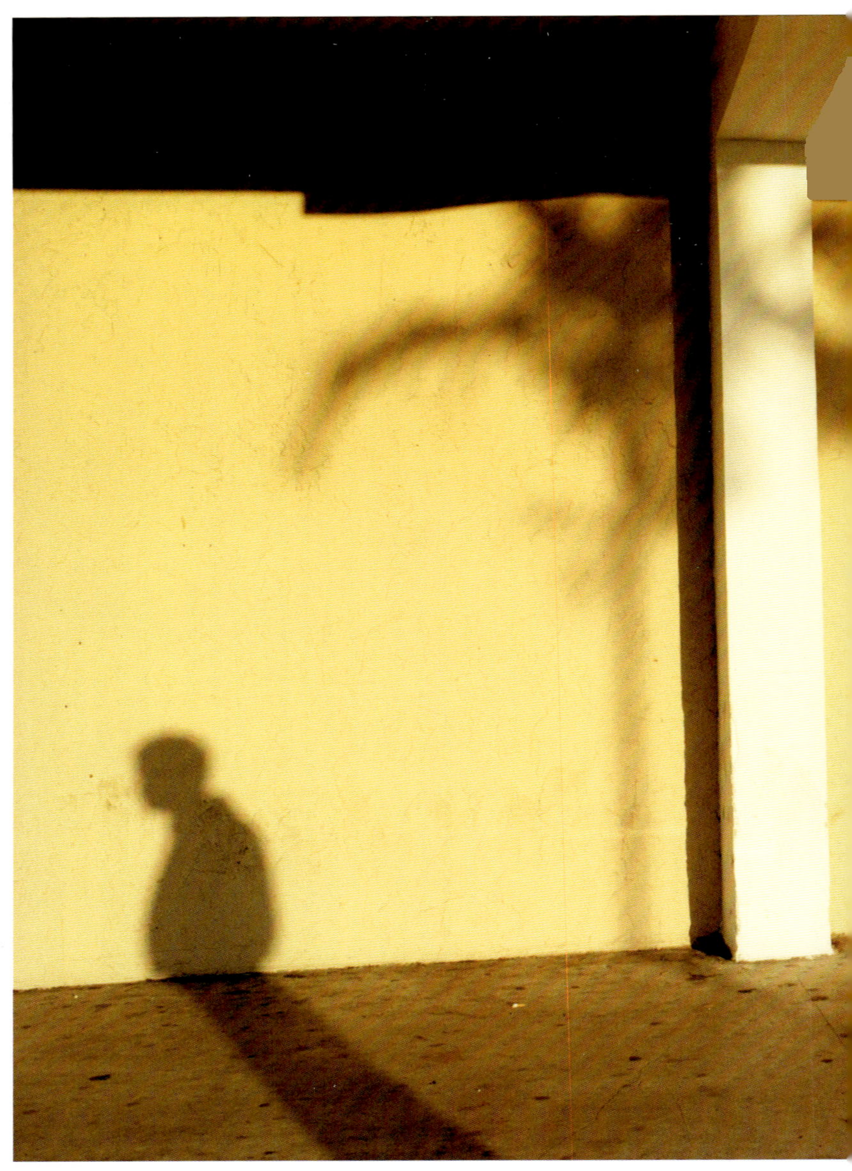

55. Guy Bourdin Archives, January 1978.

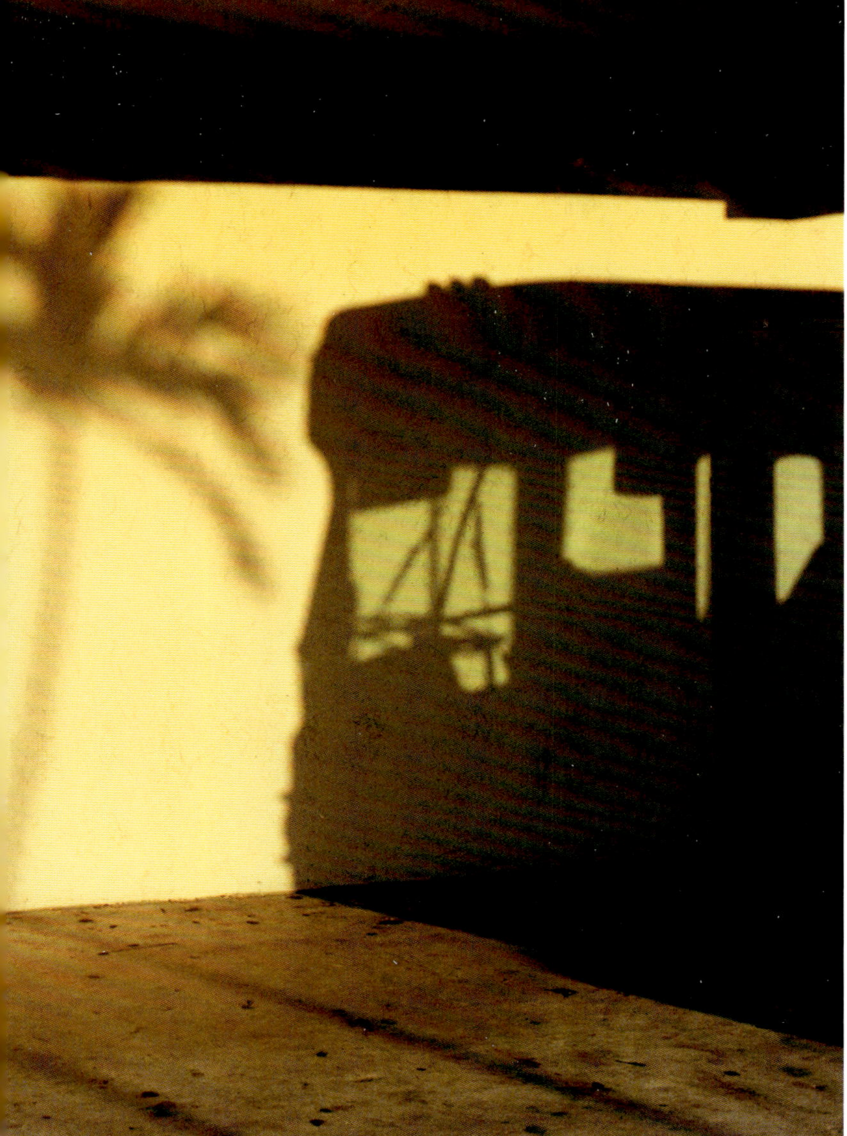

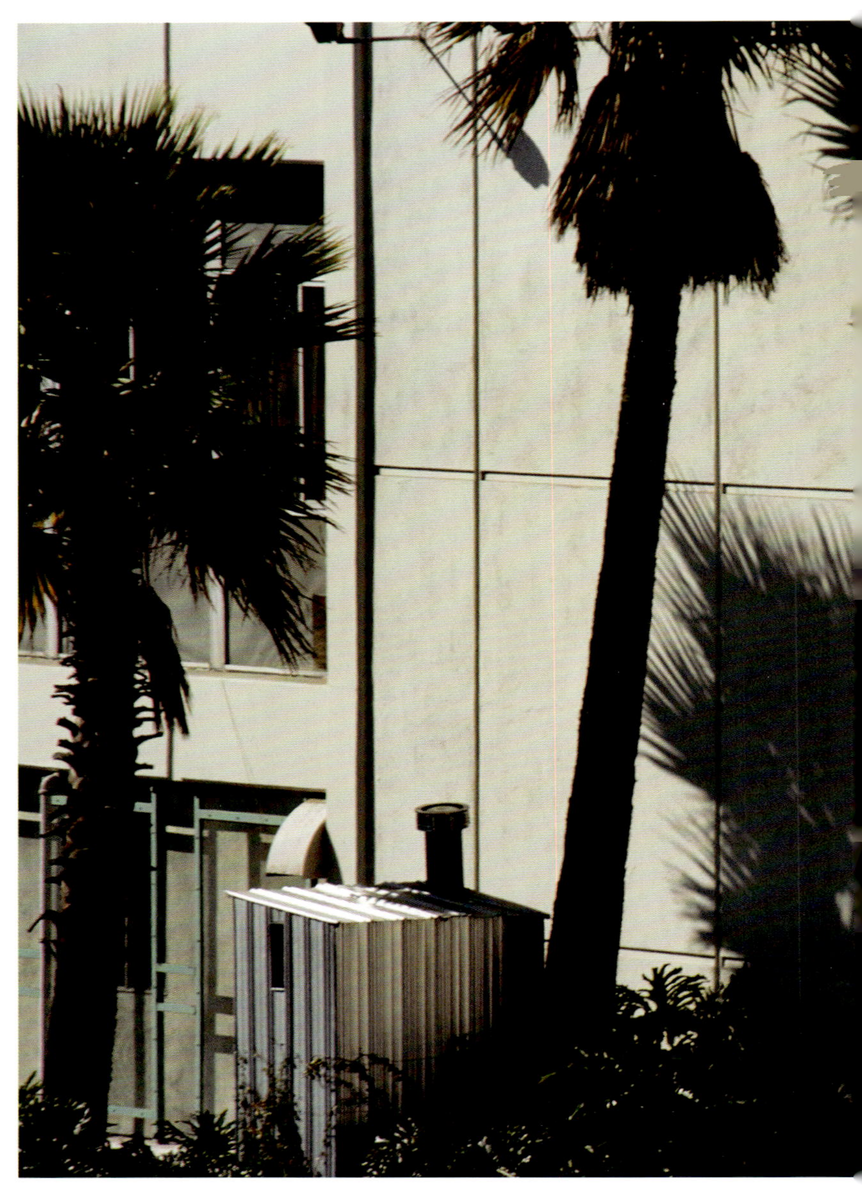

56. Guy Bourdin Archives, January 1978.

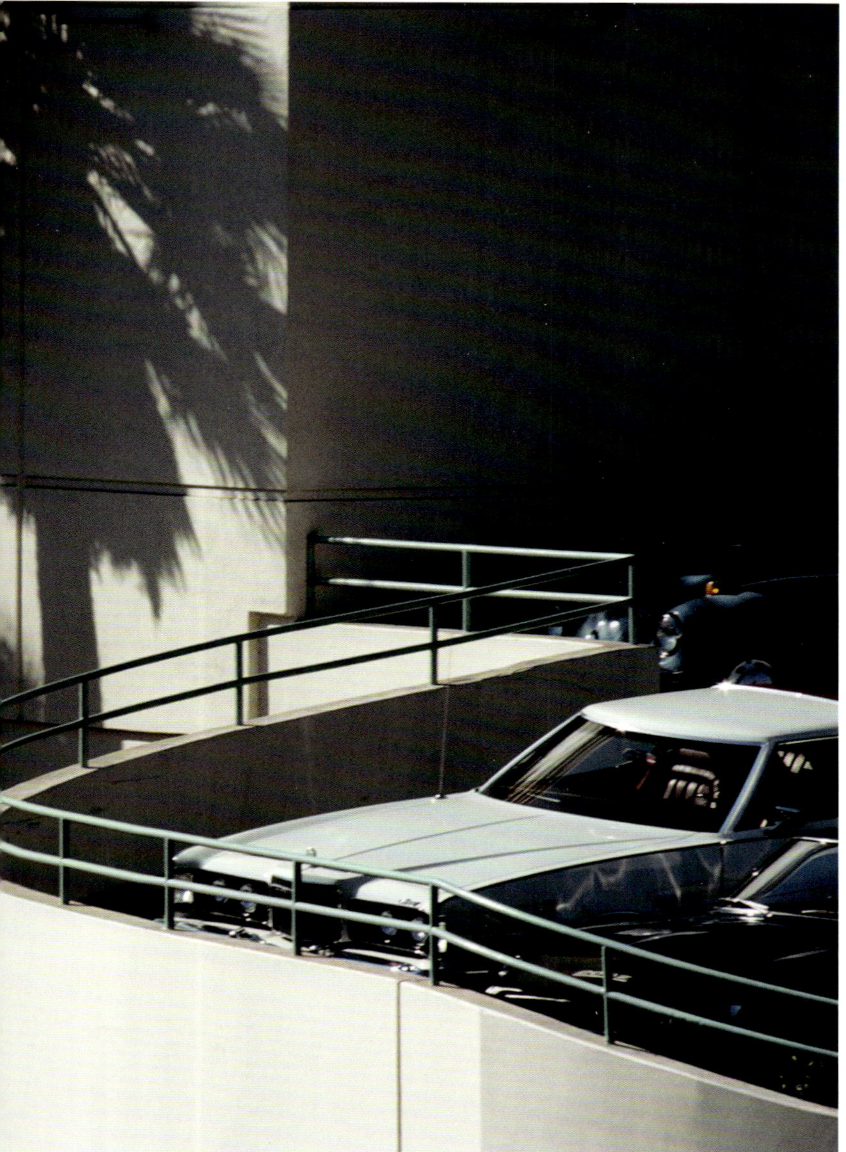

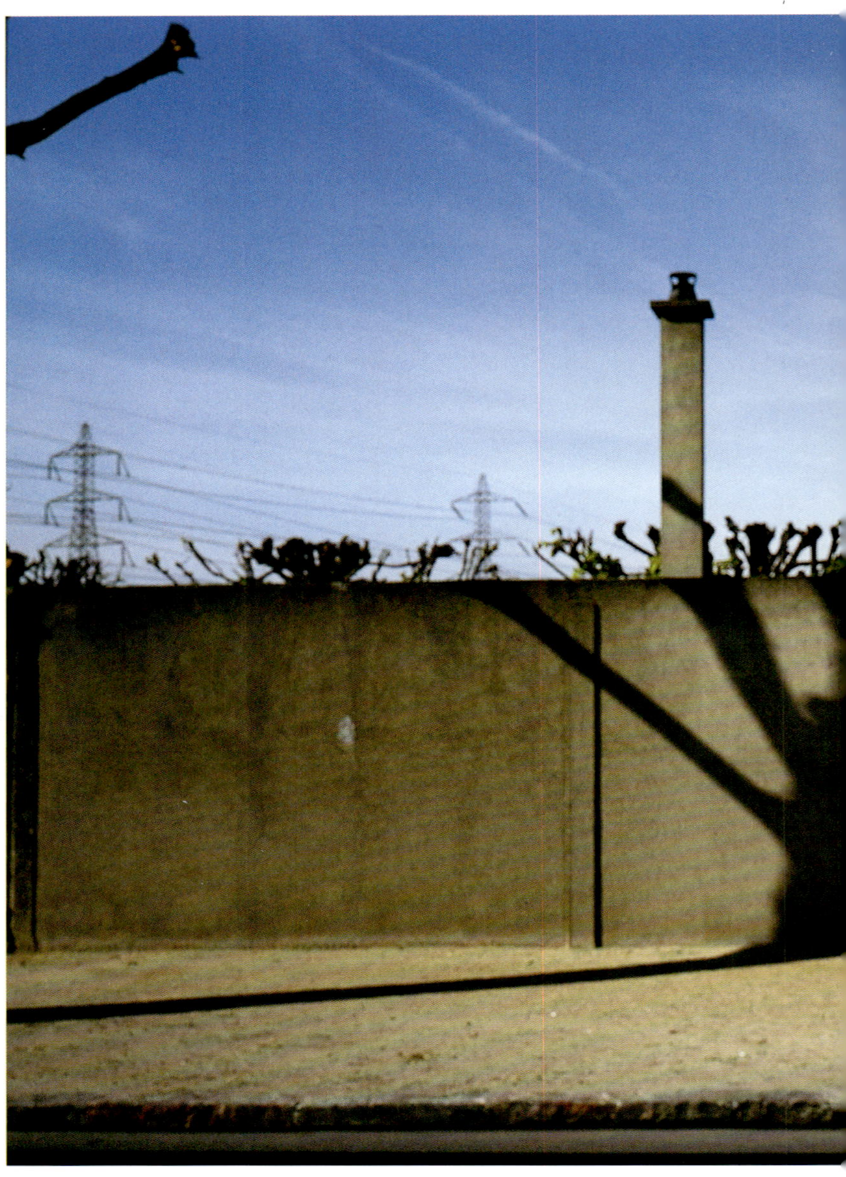

57. Guy Bourdin Archives, date unknown.

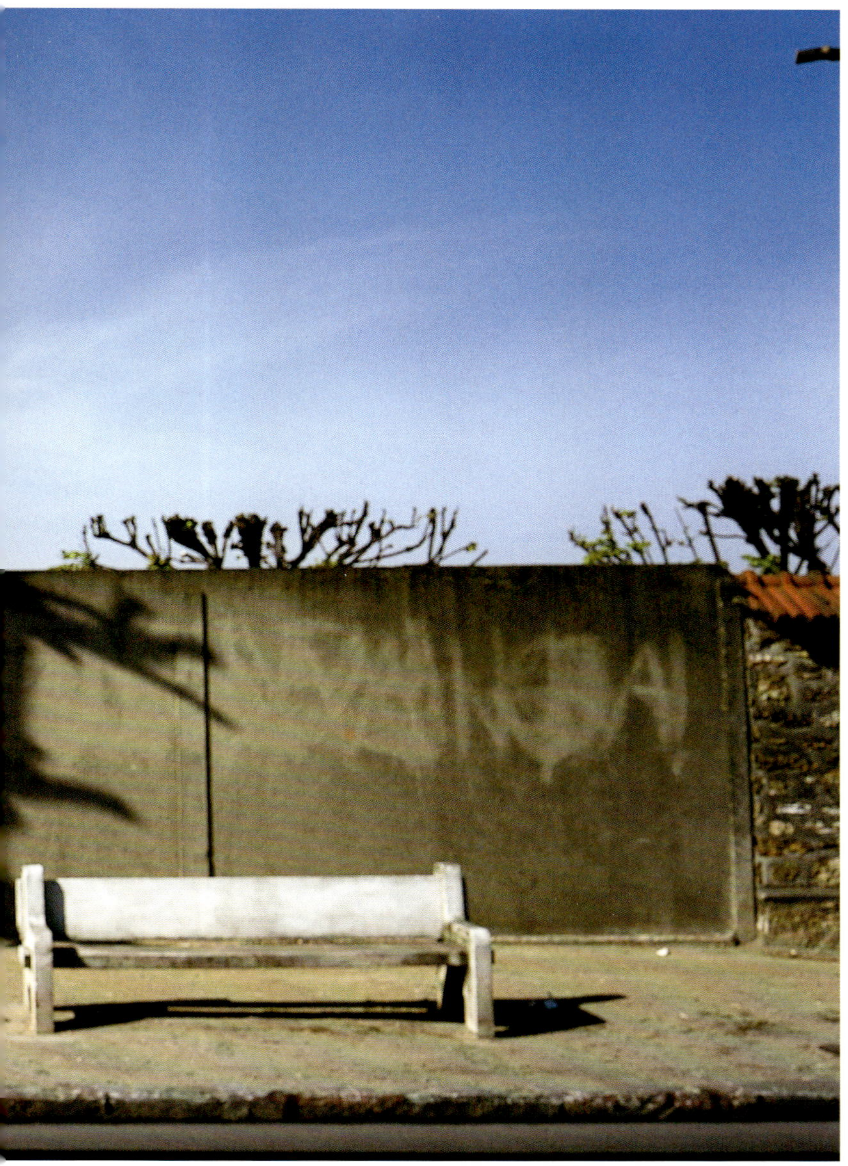

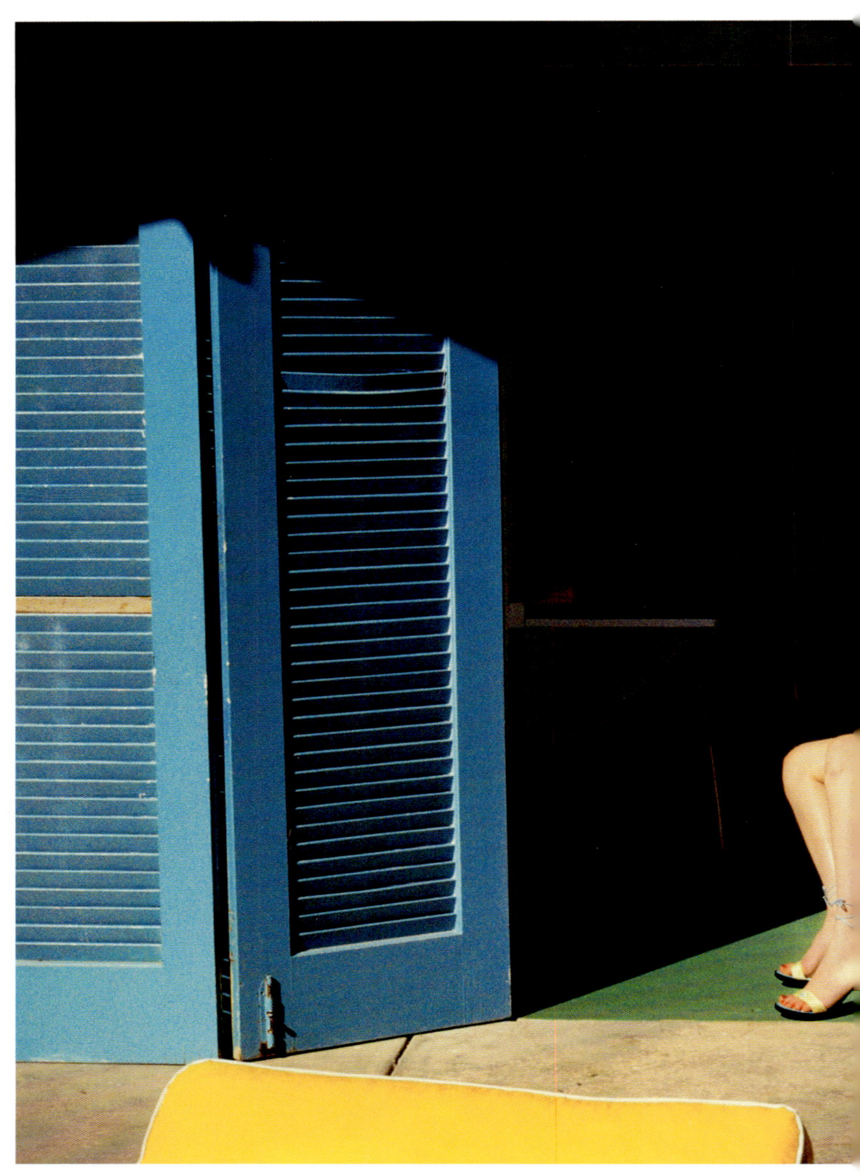
58. Campaign for Charles Jourdan, Spring 1978.

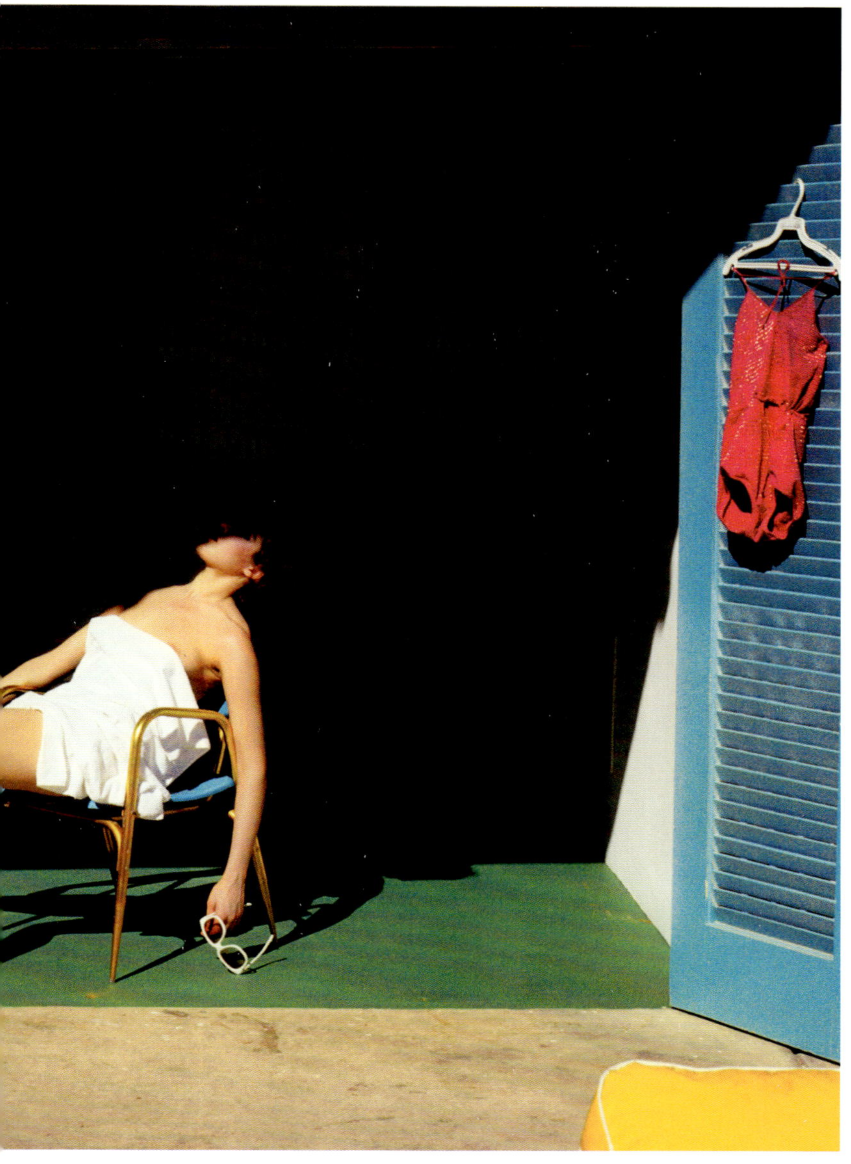

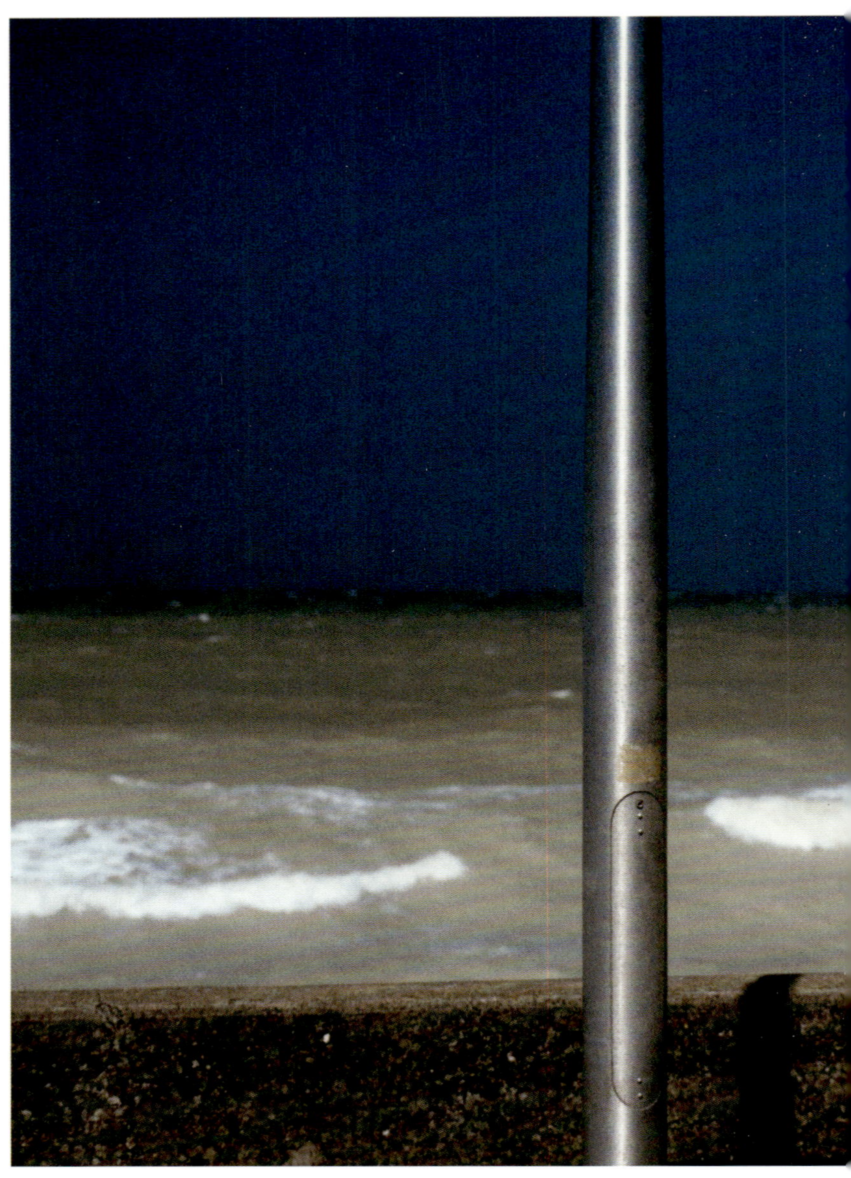

59. *Vogue France*, August 1977.

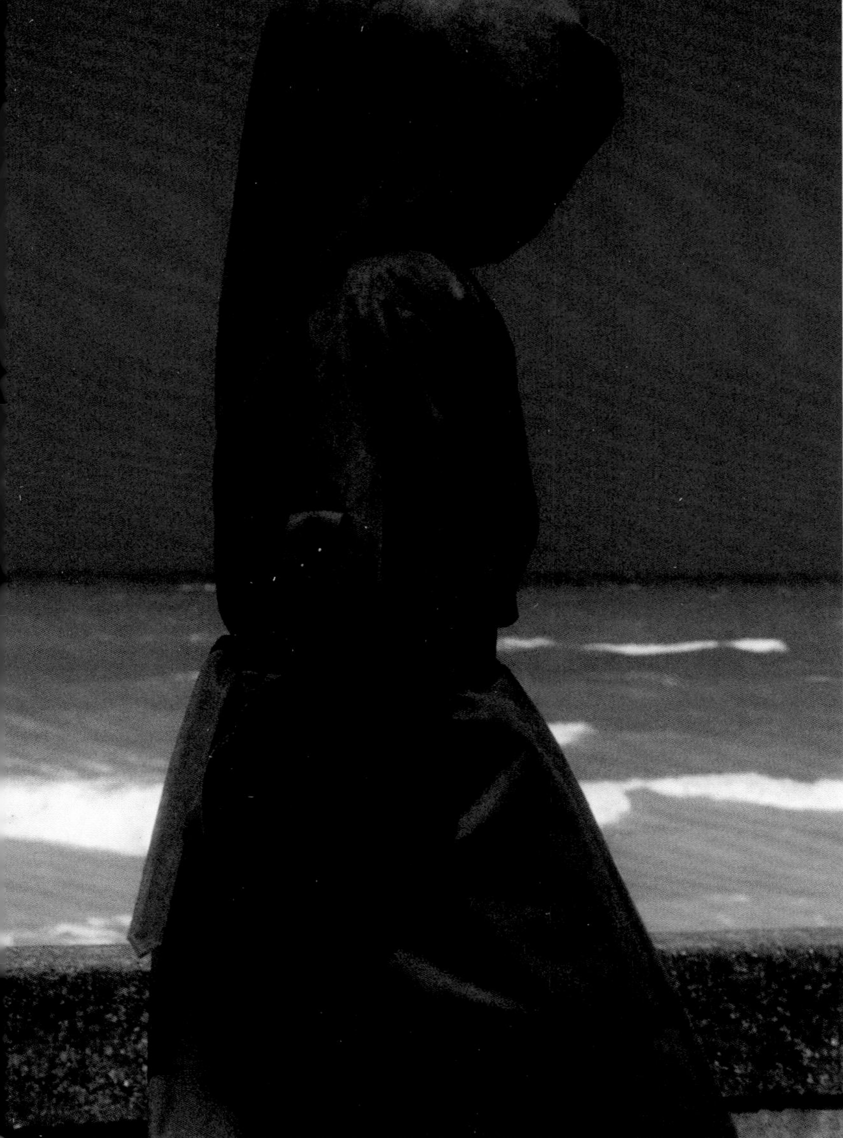

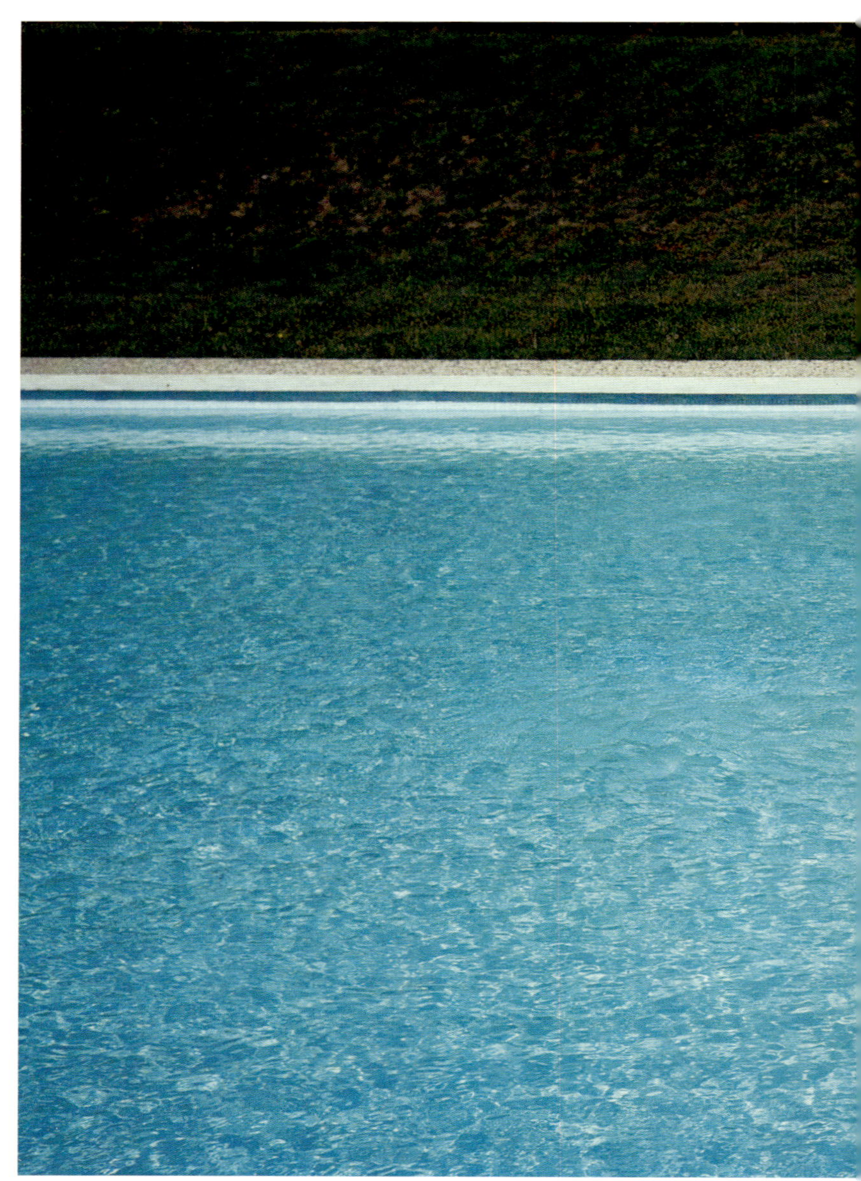

60. Unpublished, June 1975.

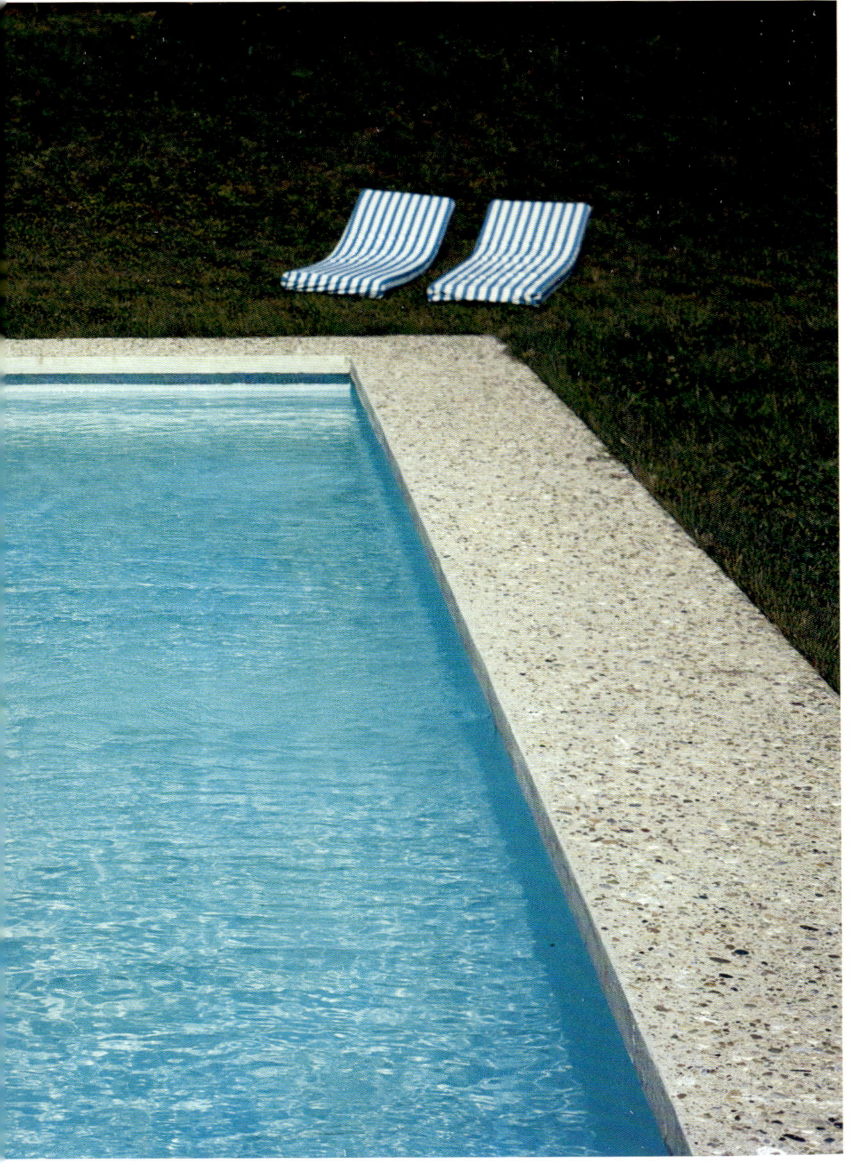

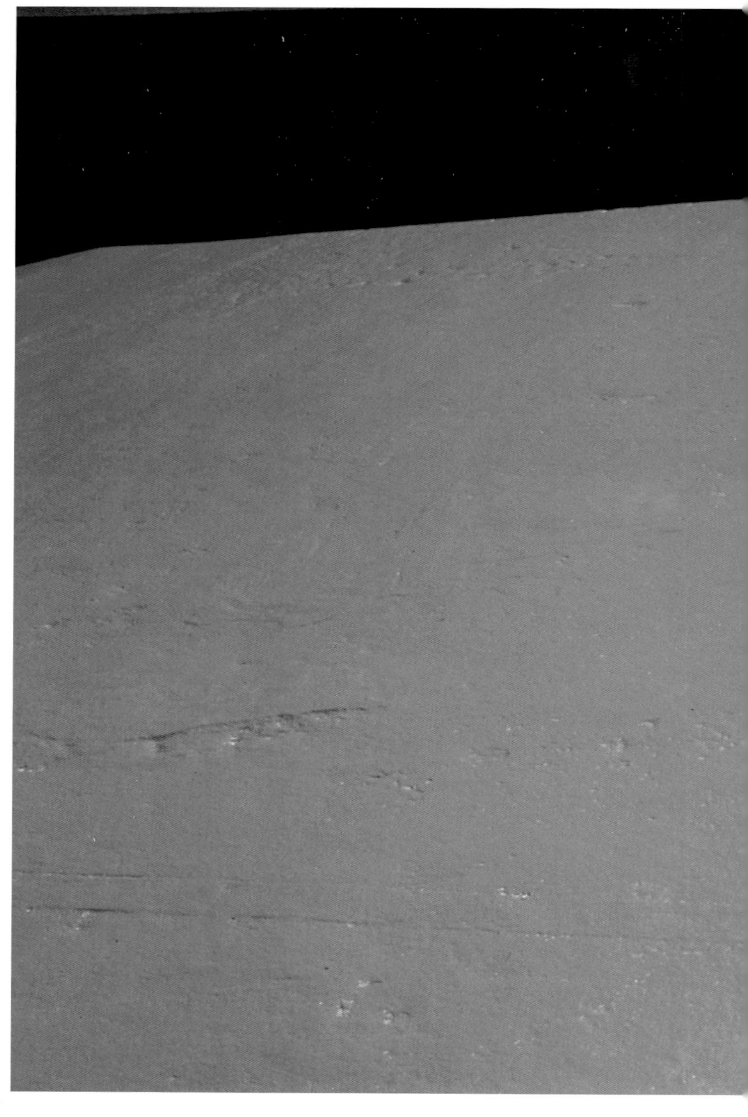

61. Guy Bourdin Archives, January 1978.

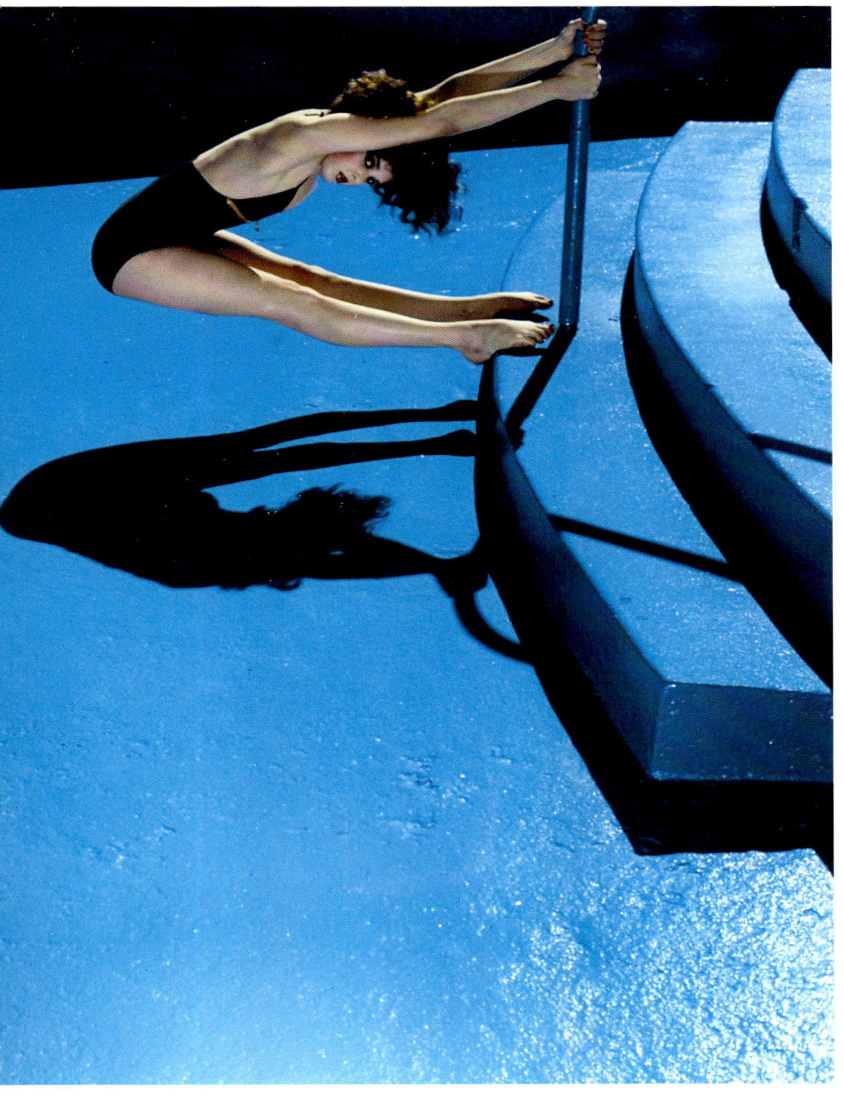

62. Campaign for Charles Jourdan, Spring 1976.

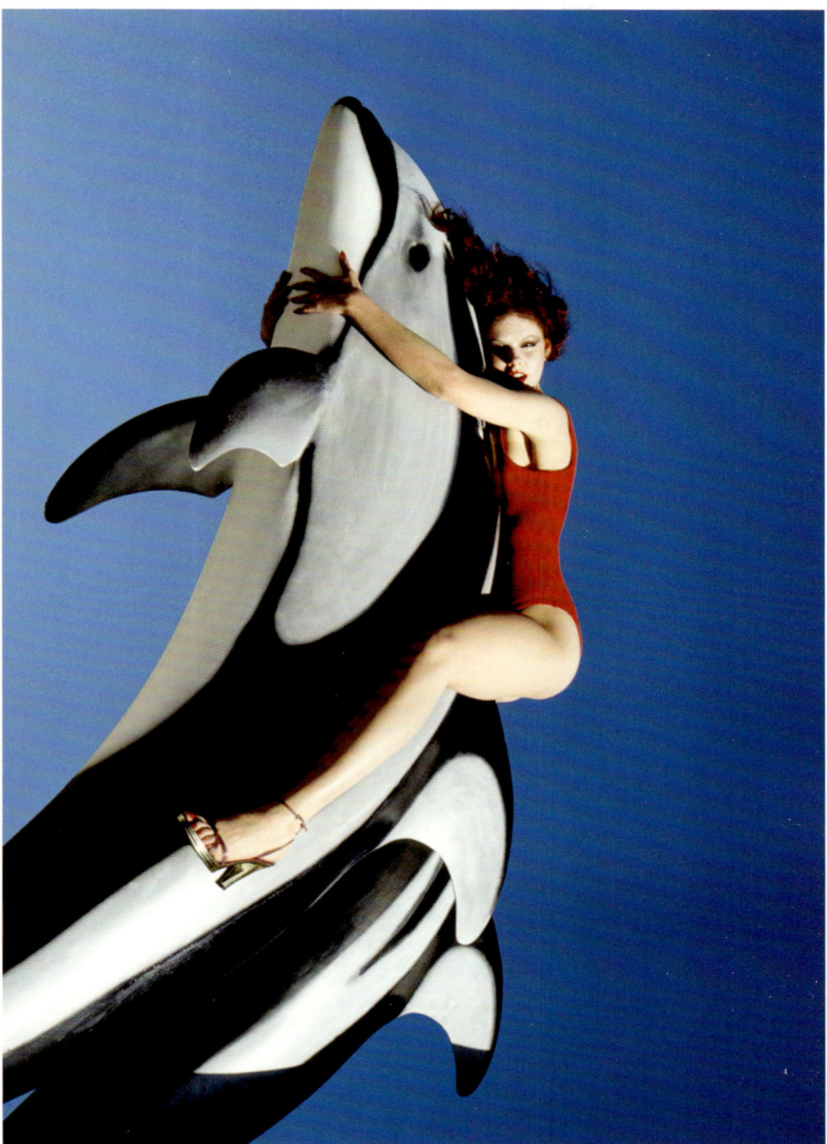

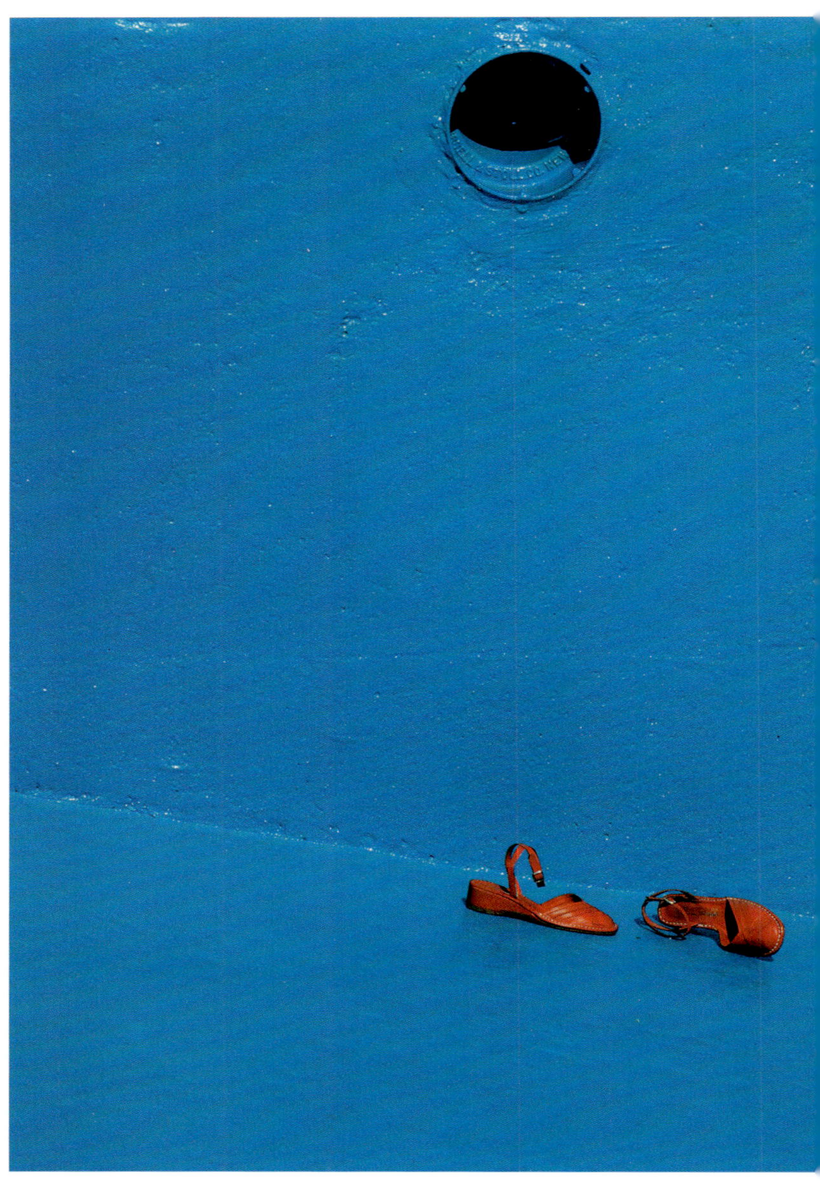

63. Campaign for Charles Jourdan, Spring 1978.

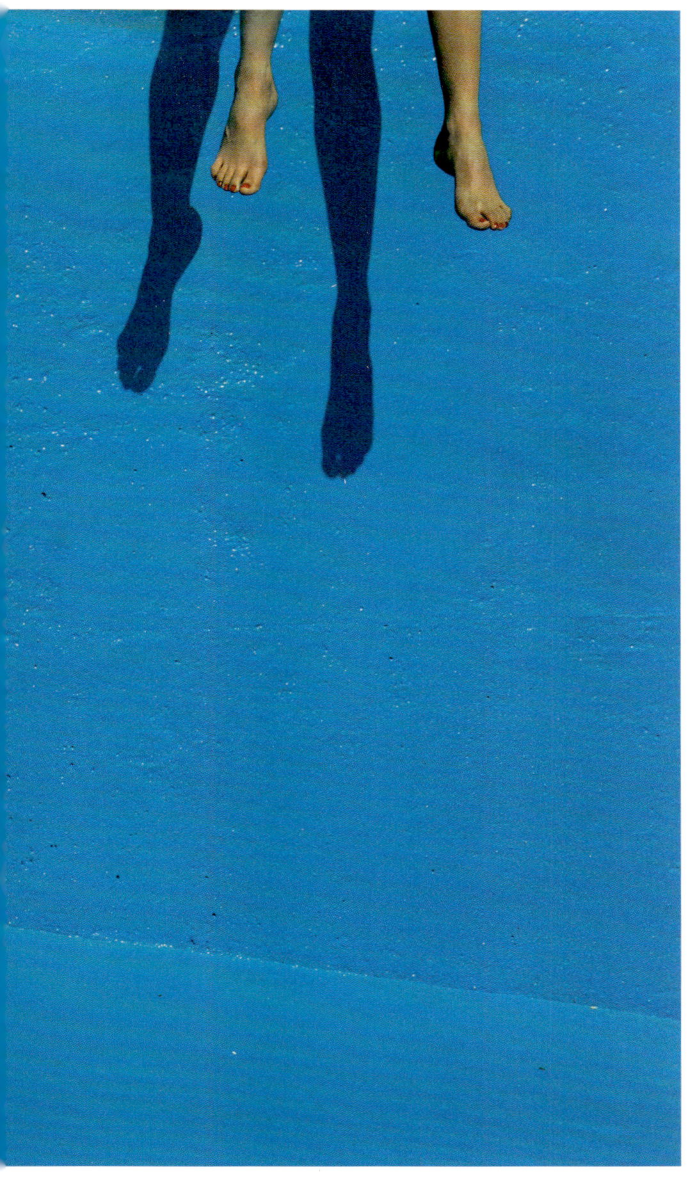

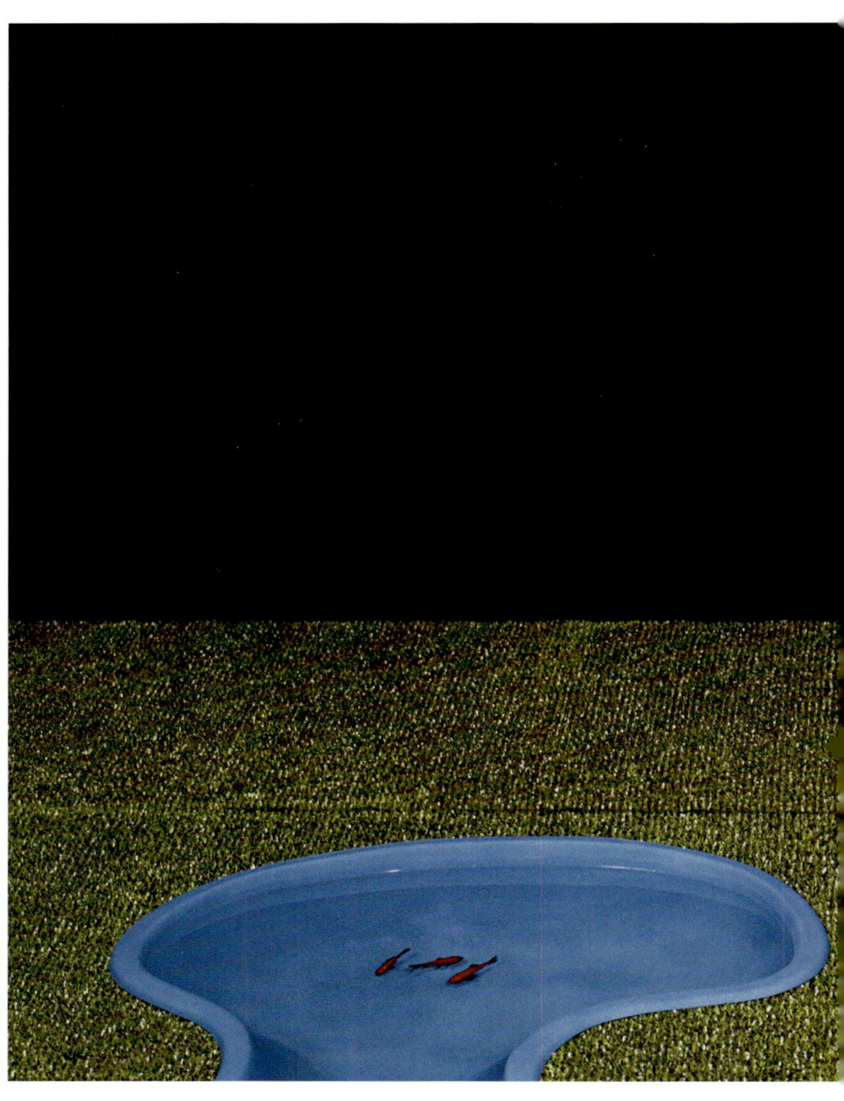

64. Campaign for Charles Jourdan, Summer 1975.

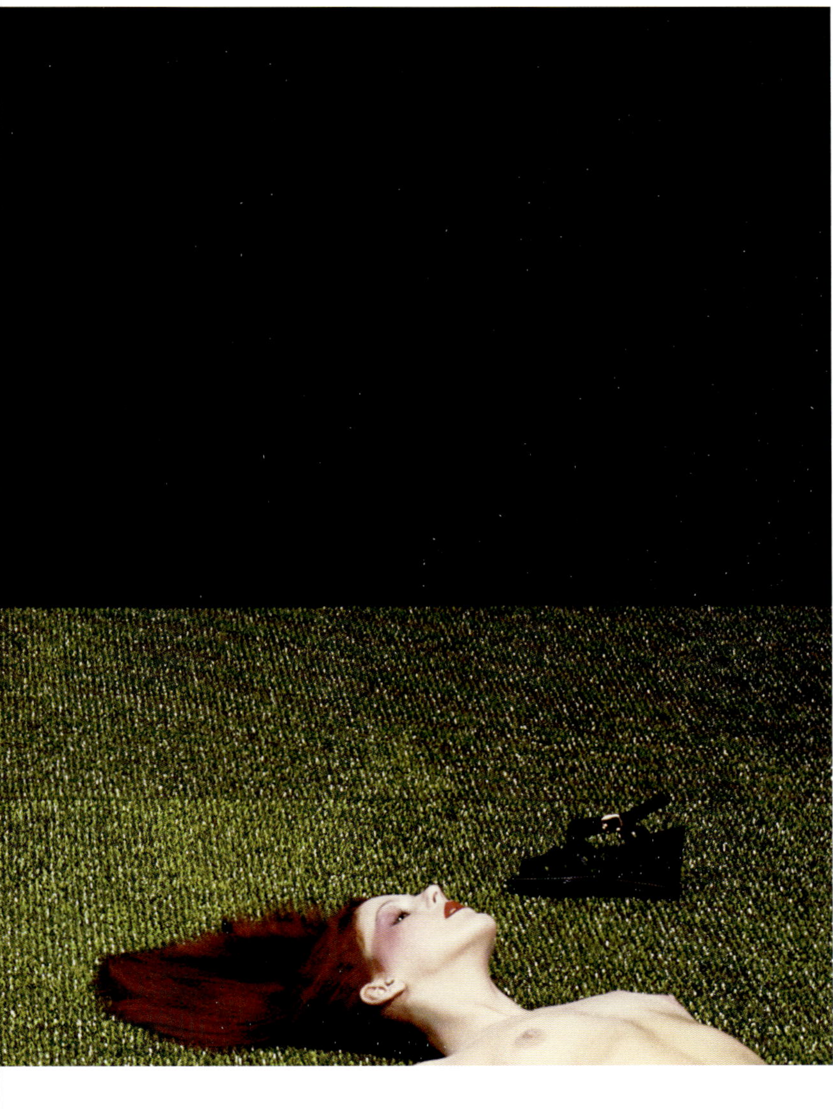

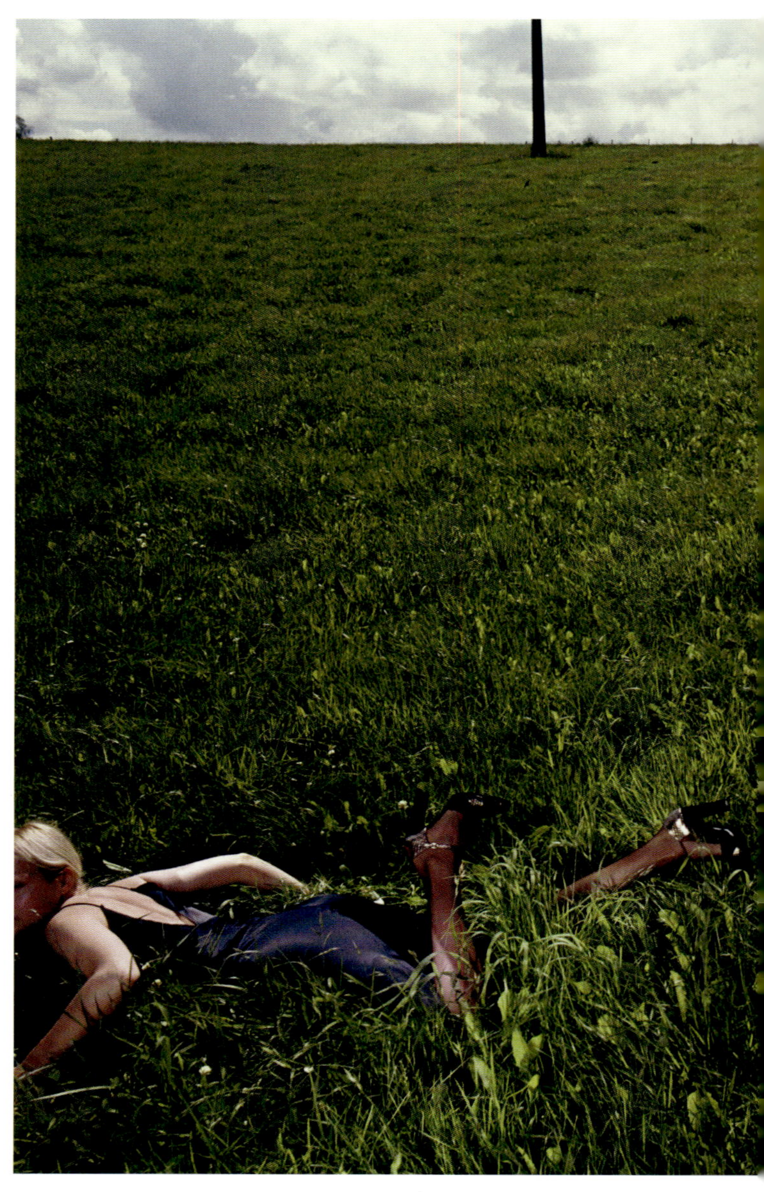

65. Campaign for Charles Jourdan, Autumn 1974.

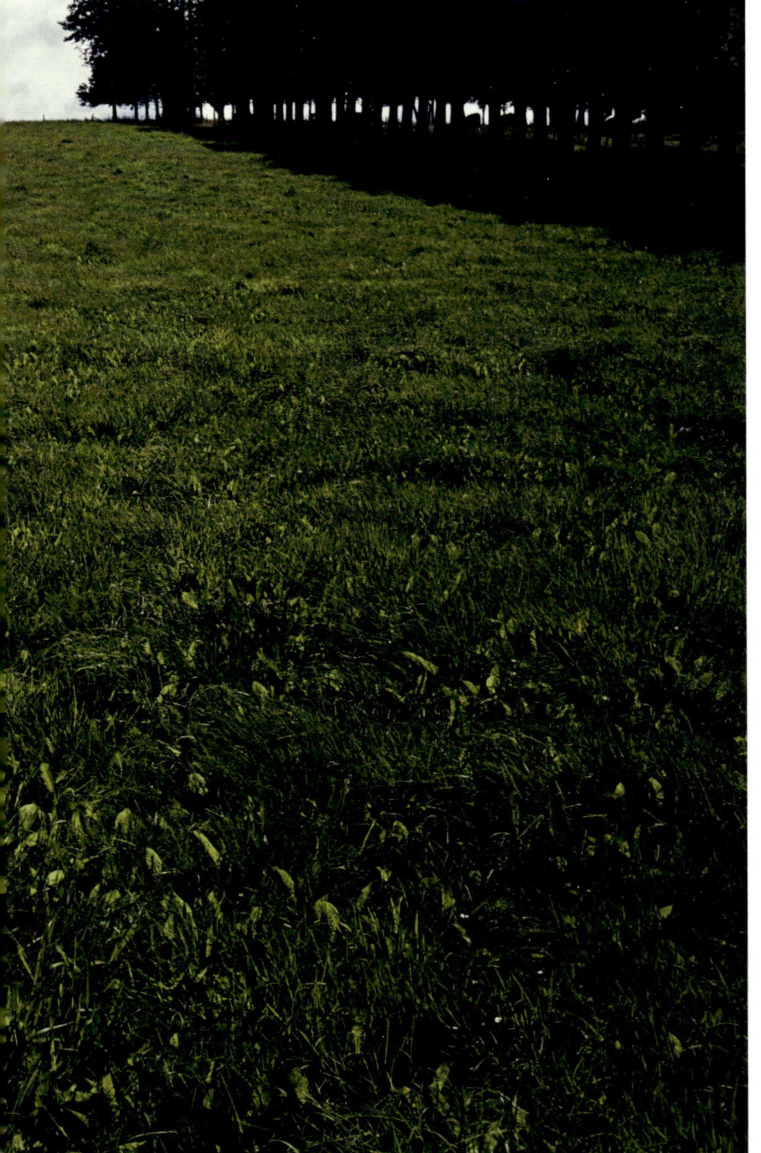

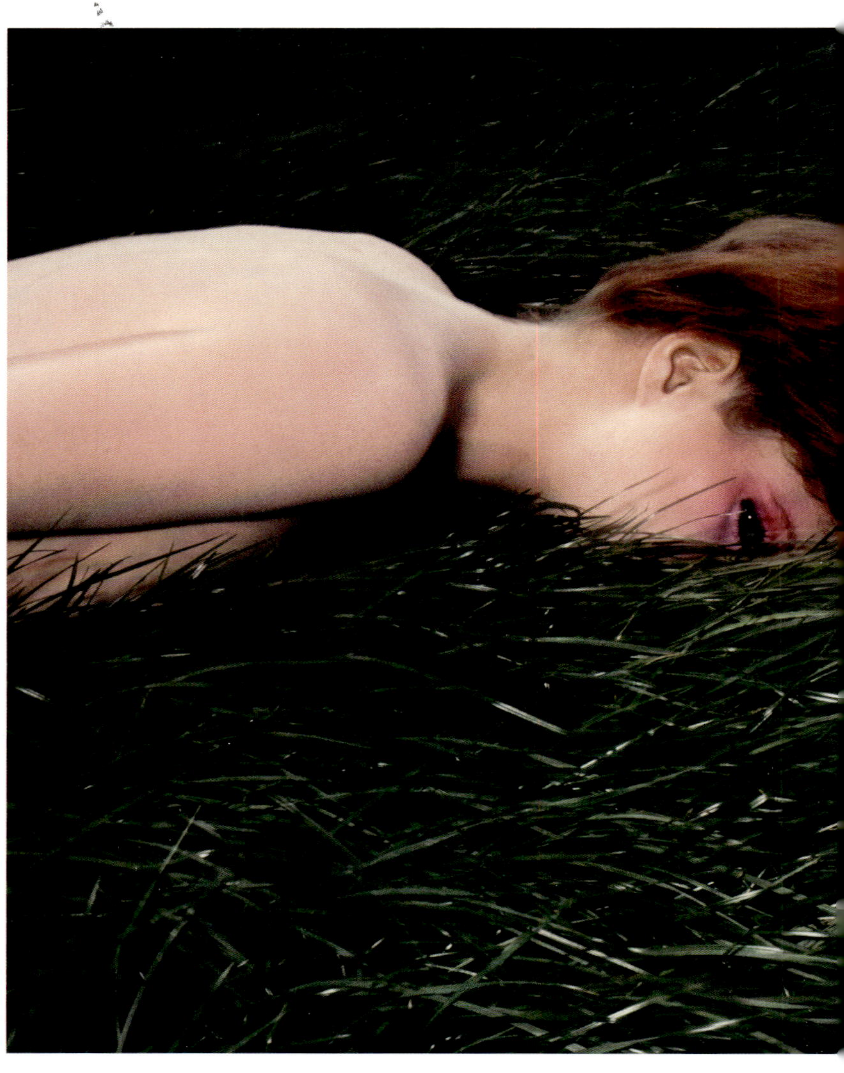

66. *20 ans*, c. 1977.

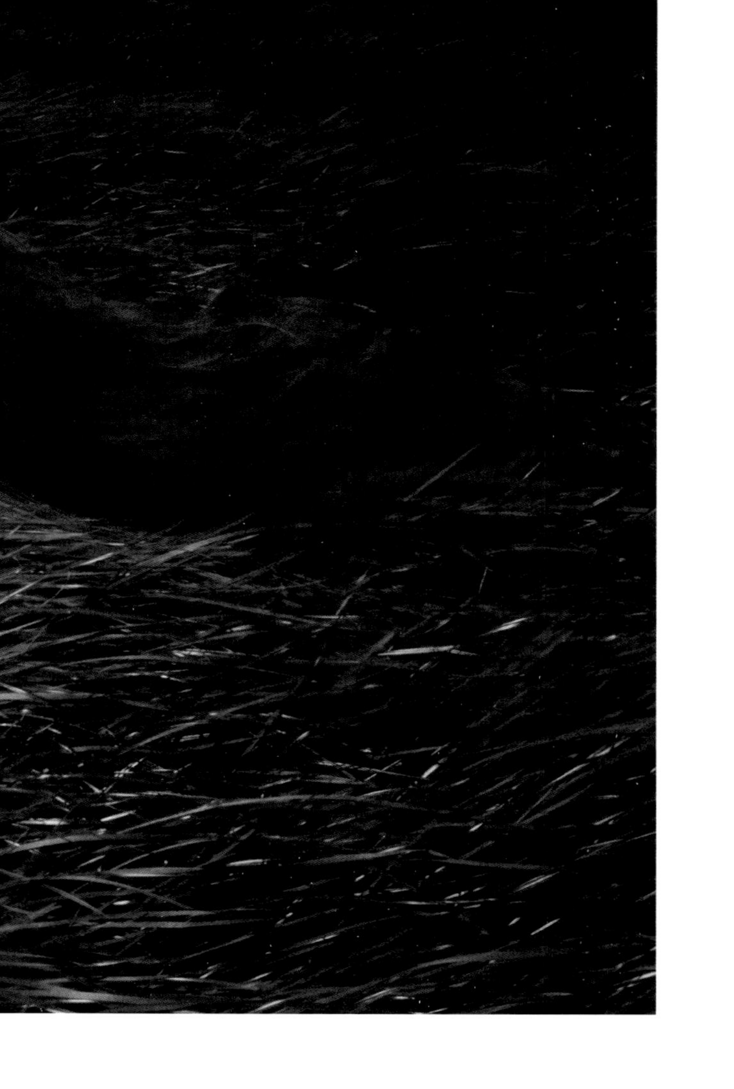

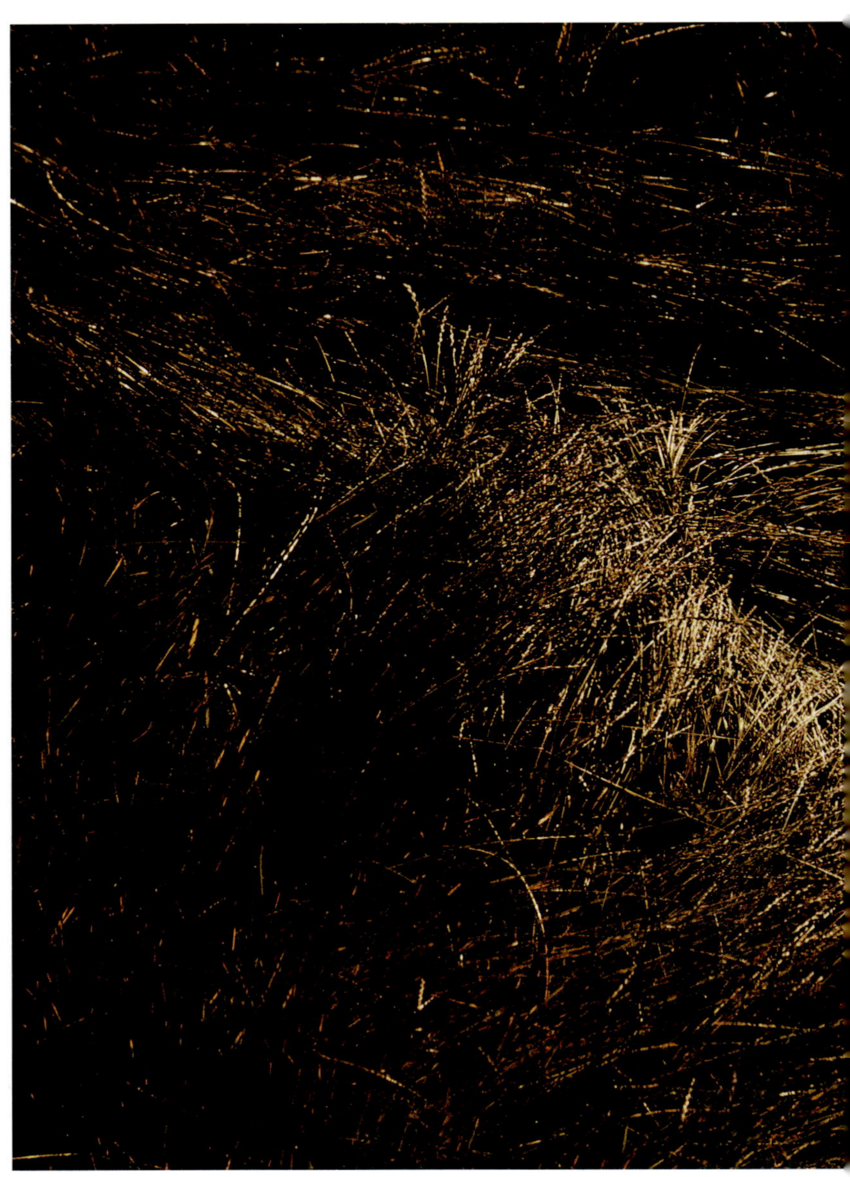

67. Unpublished, October 1977.

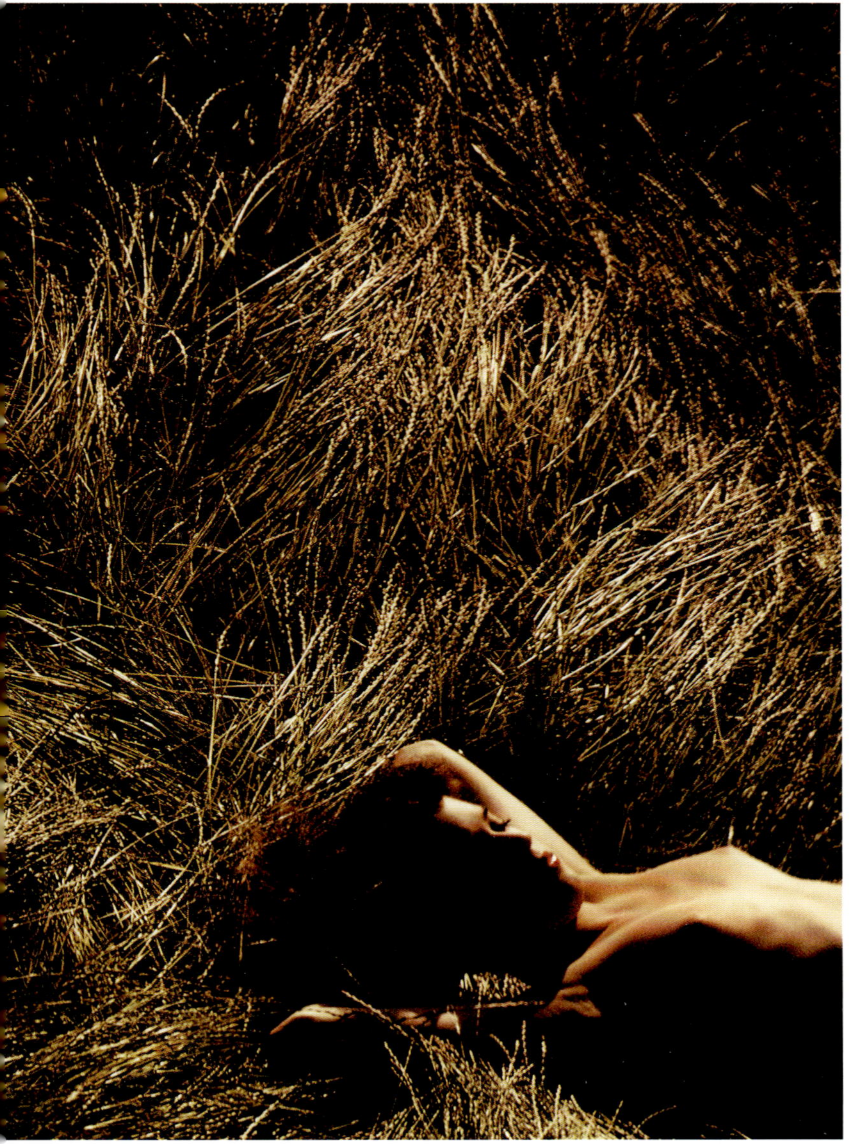

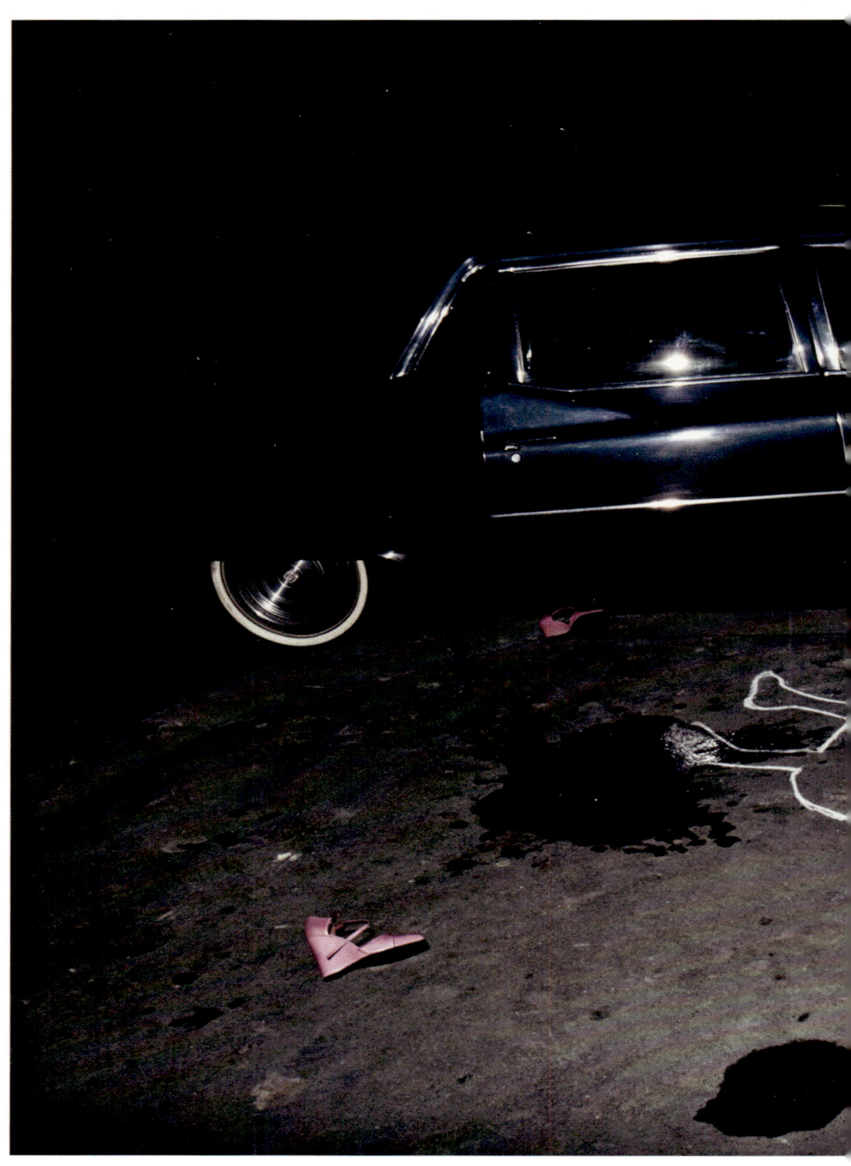

68. Campaign for Charles Jourdan, Spring 1975.

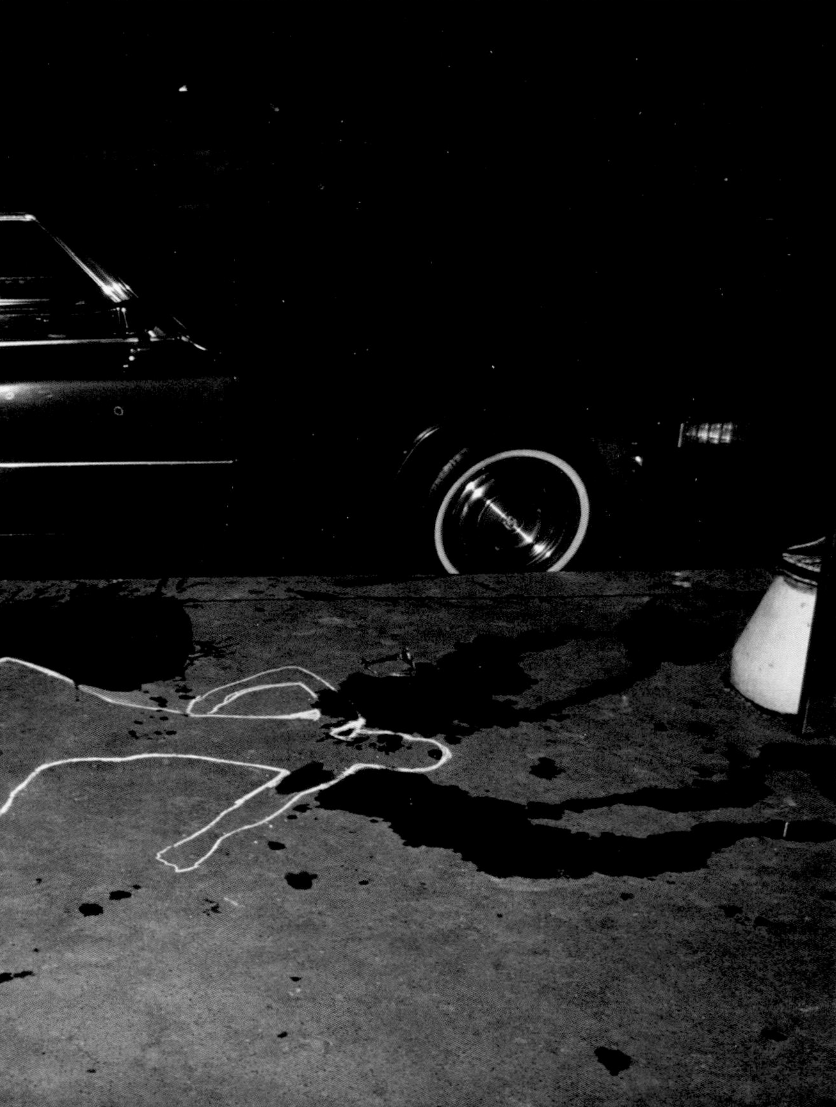

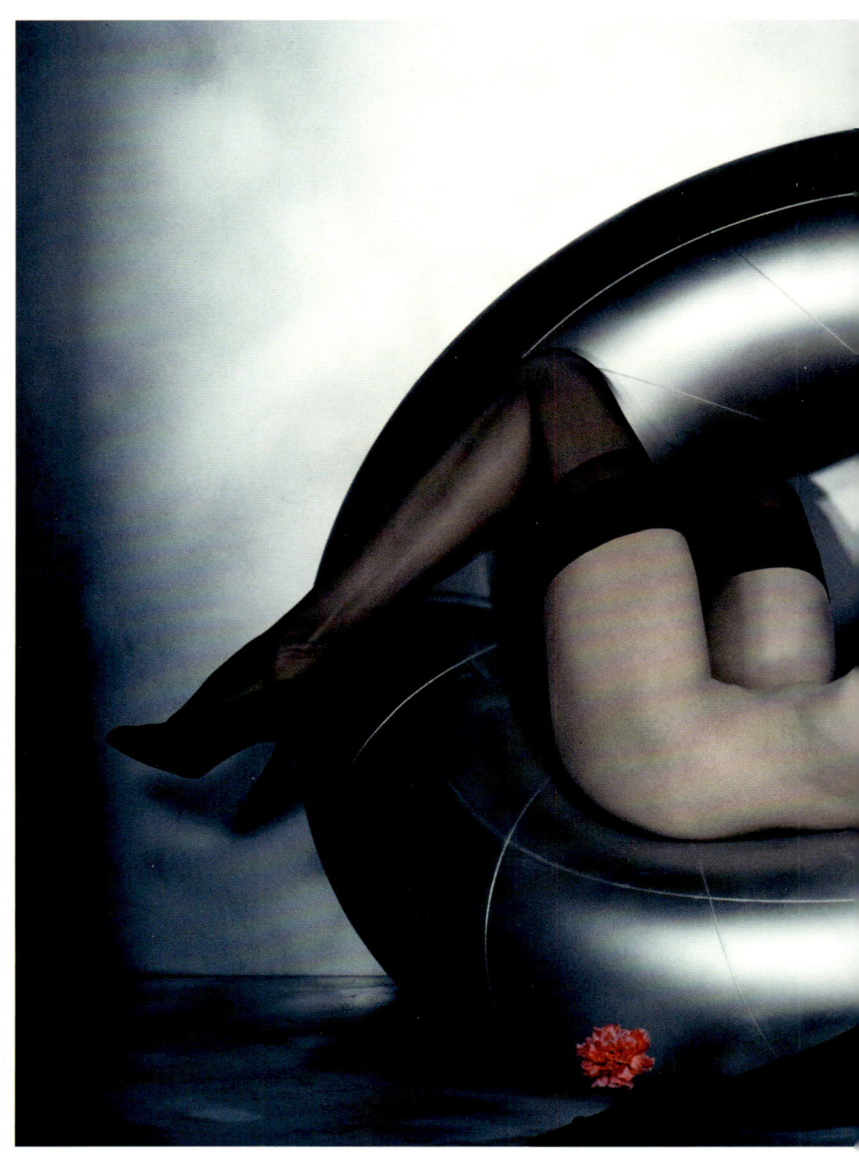

69. Pentax Calendar, 1980.

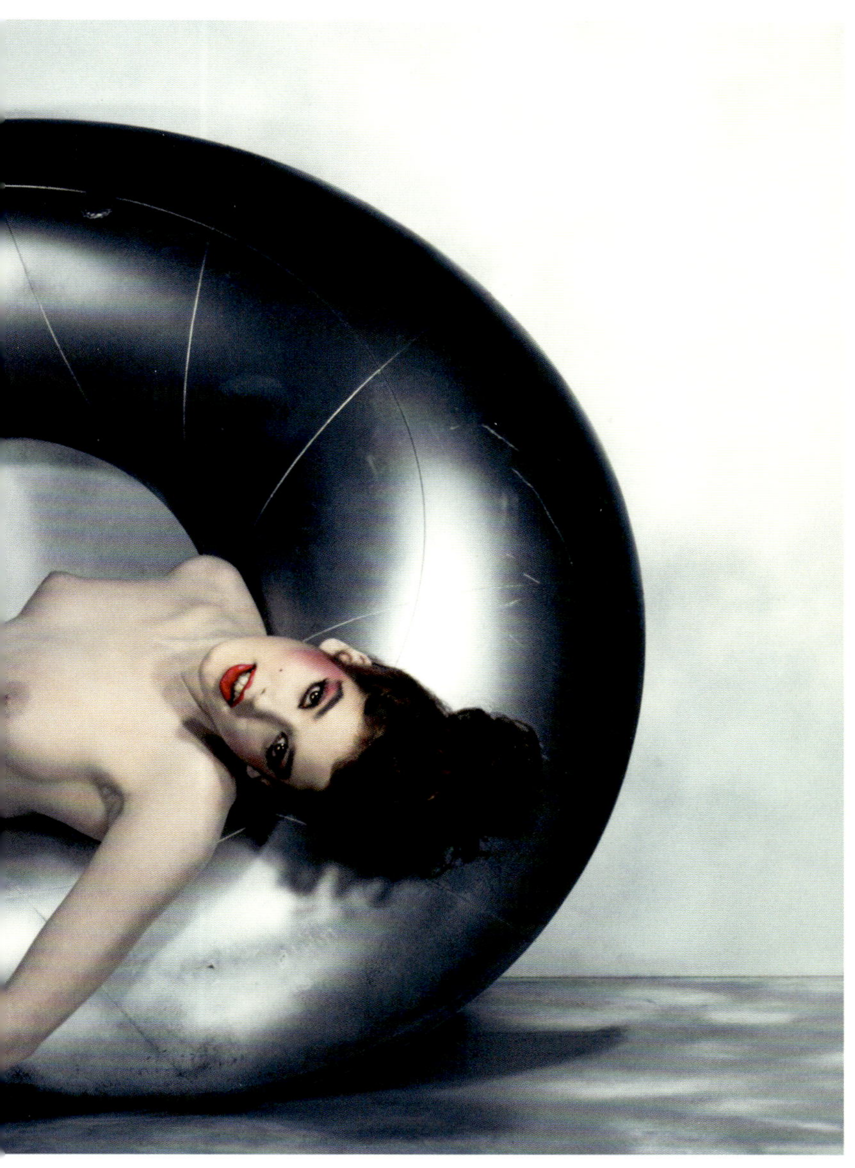

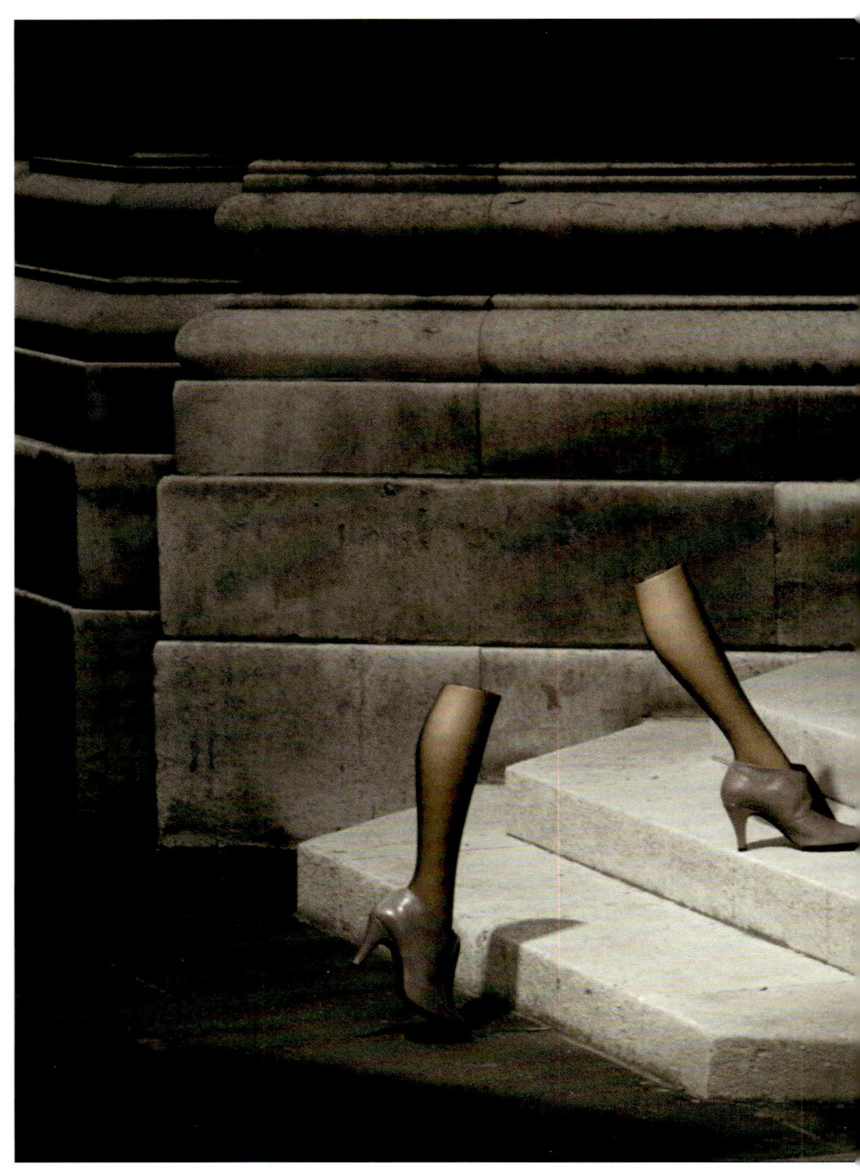

70. Campaign for Charles Jourdan, Autumn 1978.

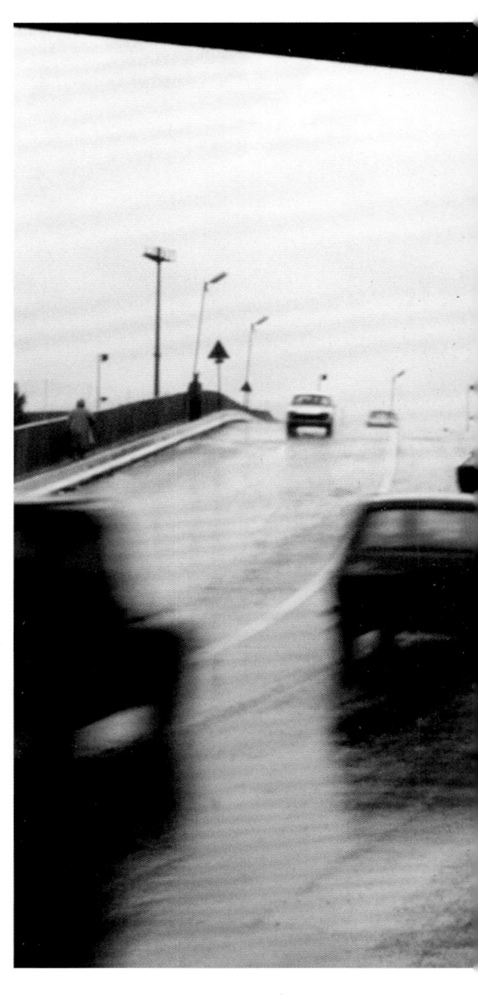

71. *Vogue France*, November 1975.

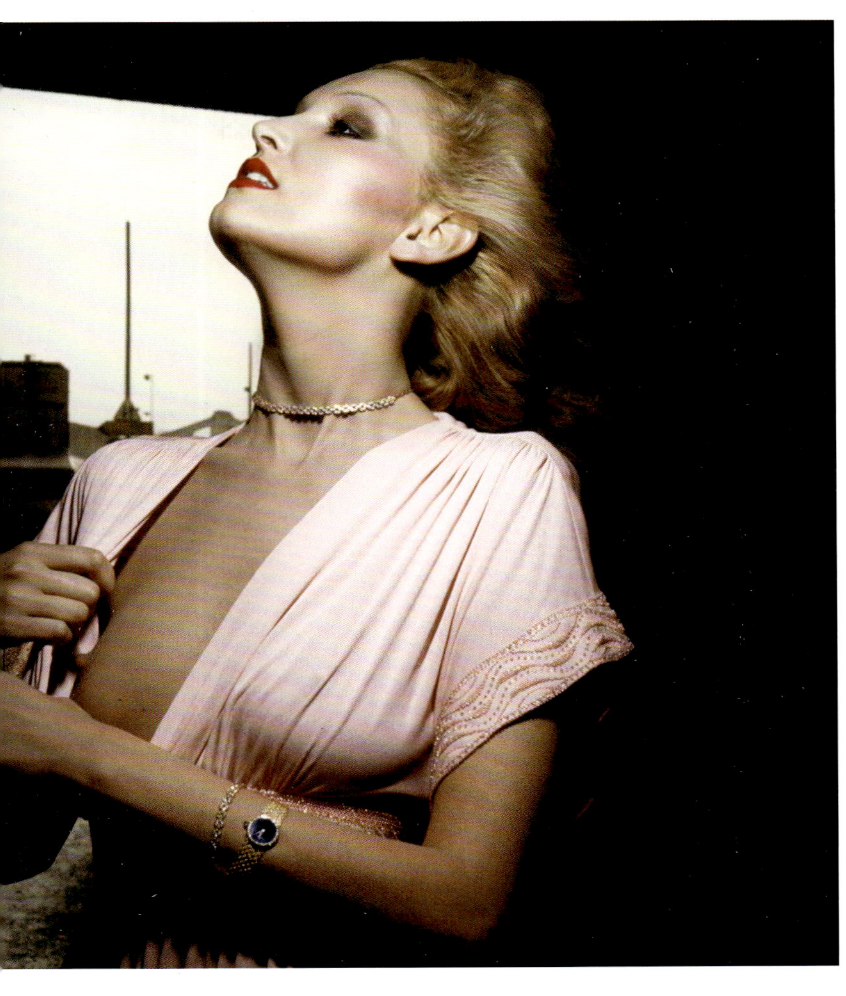

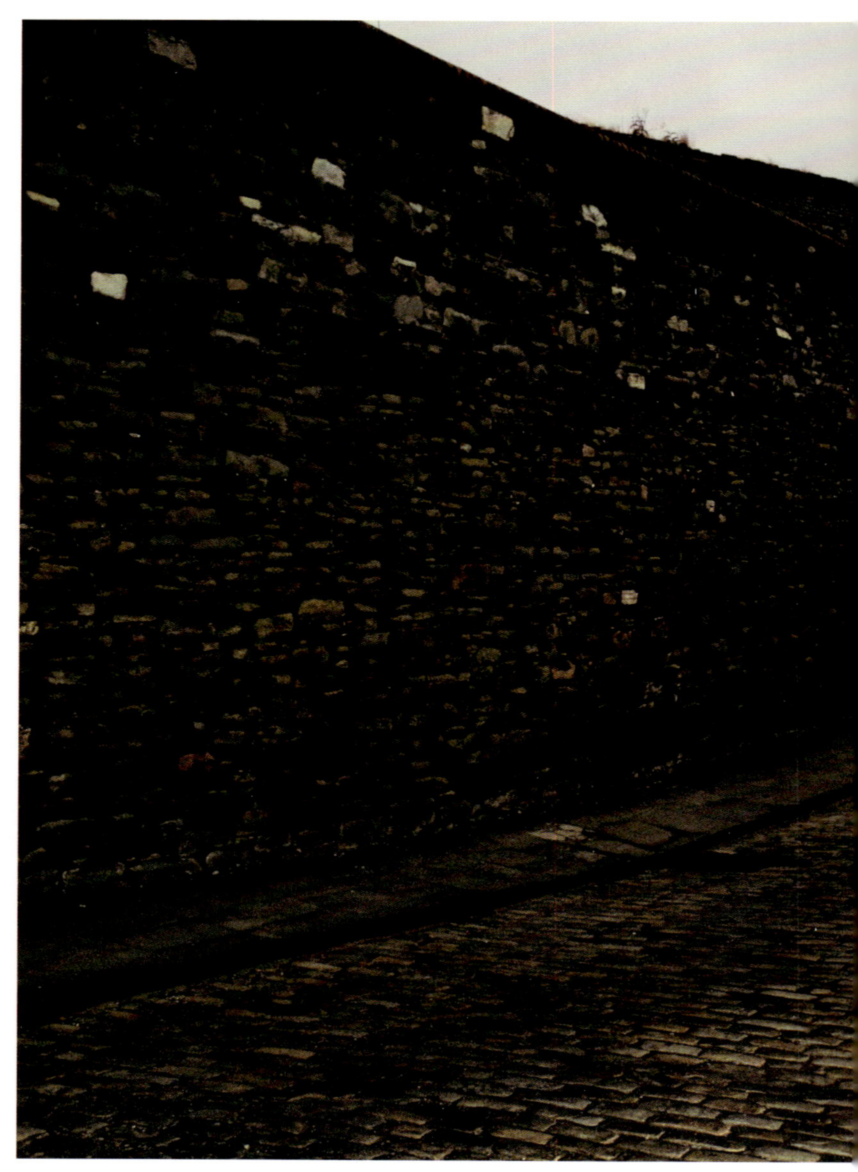

72. Unpublished, September 1979.

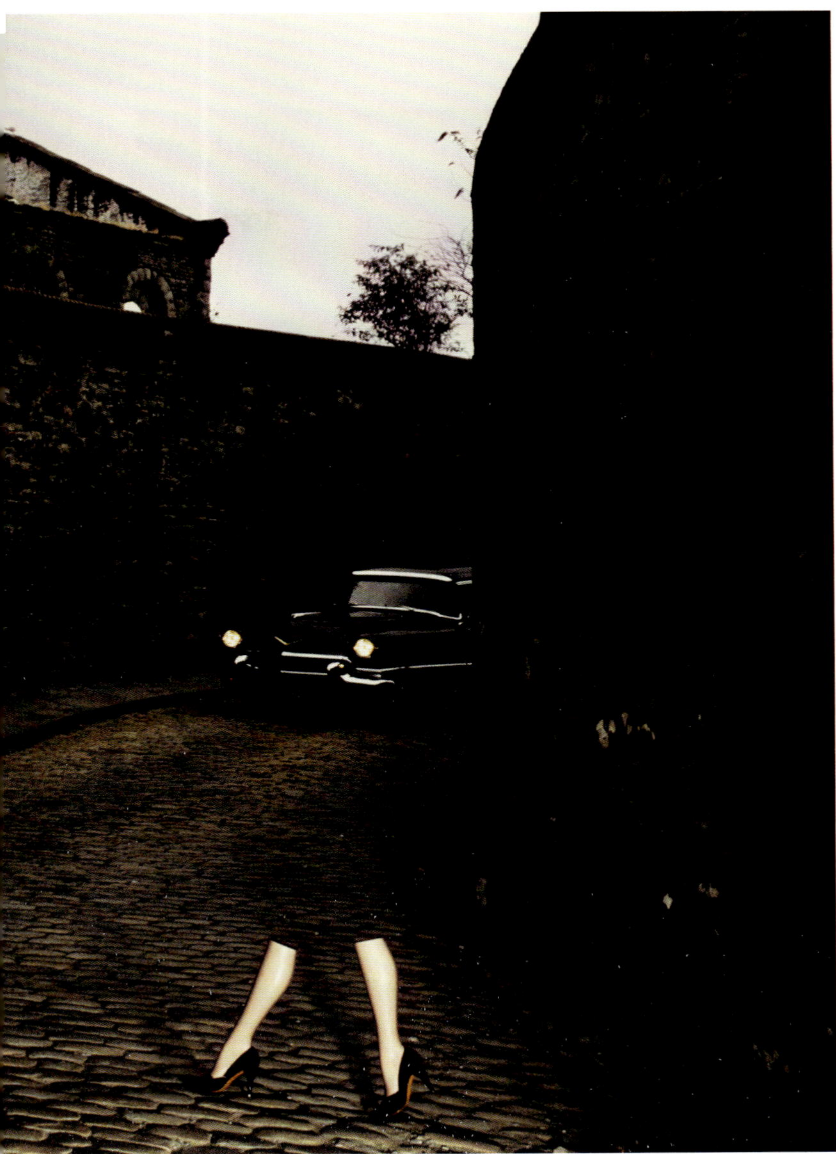

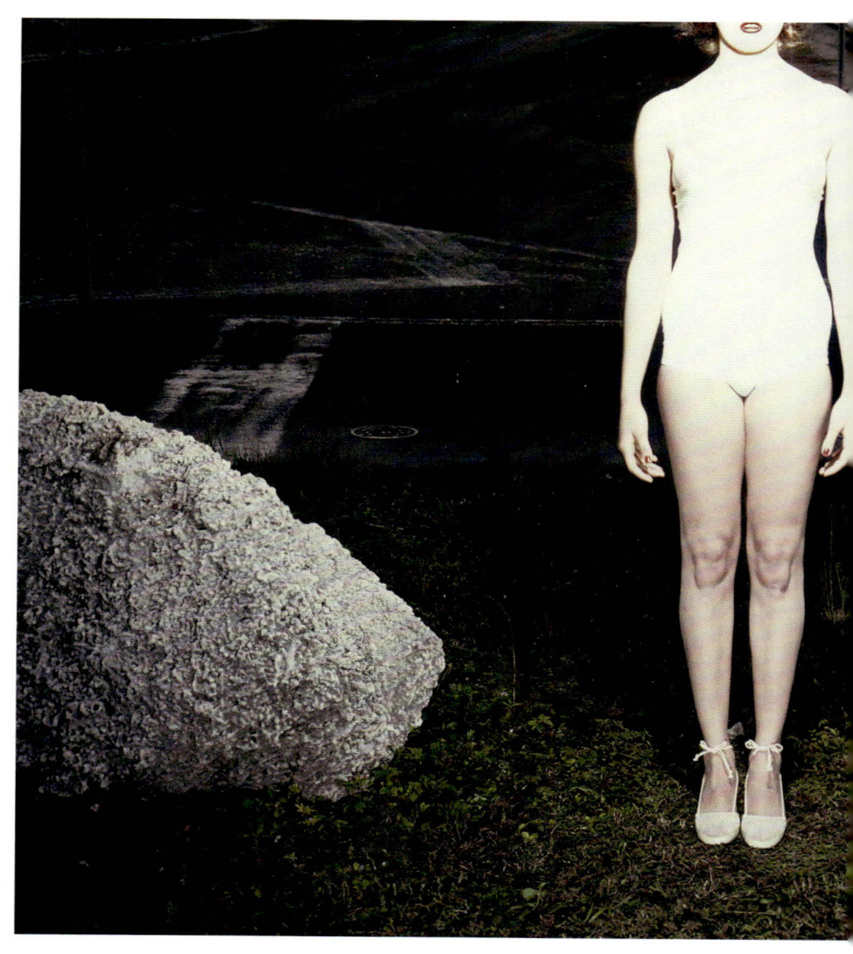
73. Campaign for Charles Jourdan, Spring 1978.

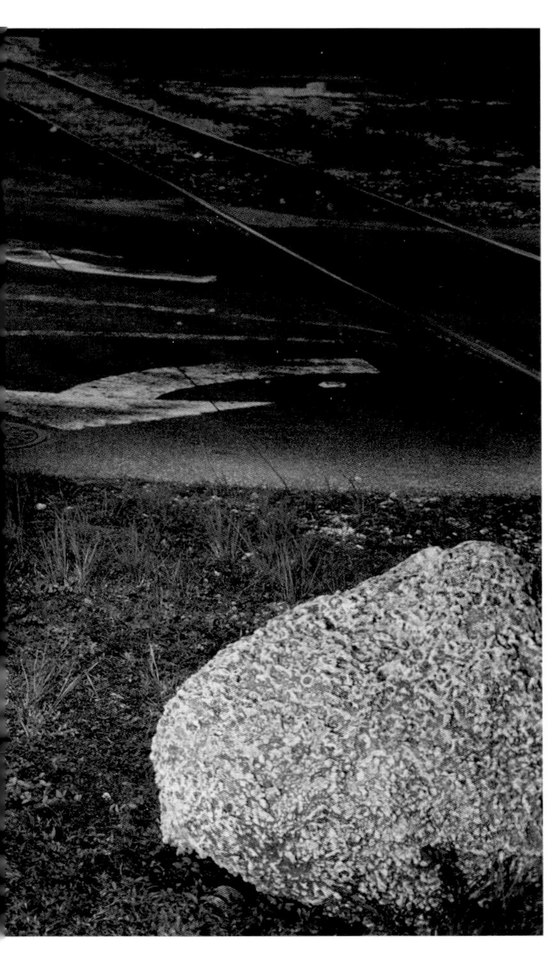

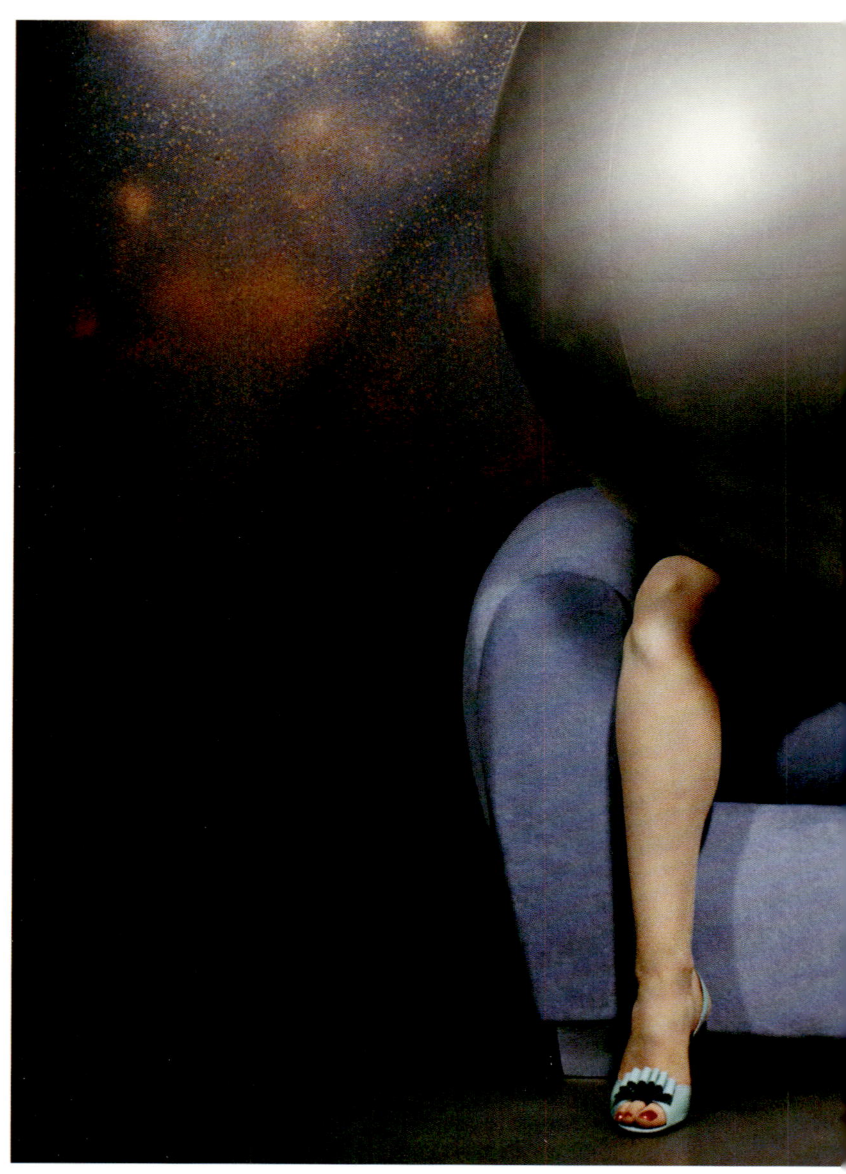

74. Campaign for Charles Jourdan, Spring 1980.

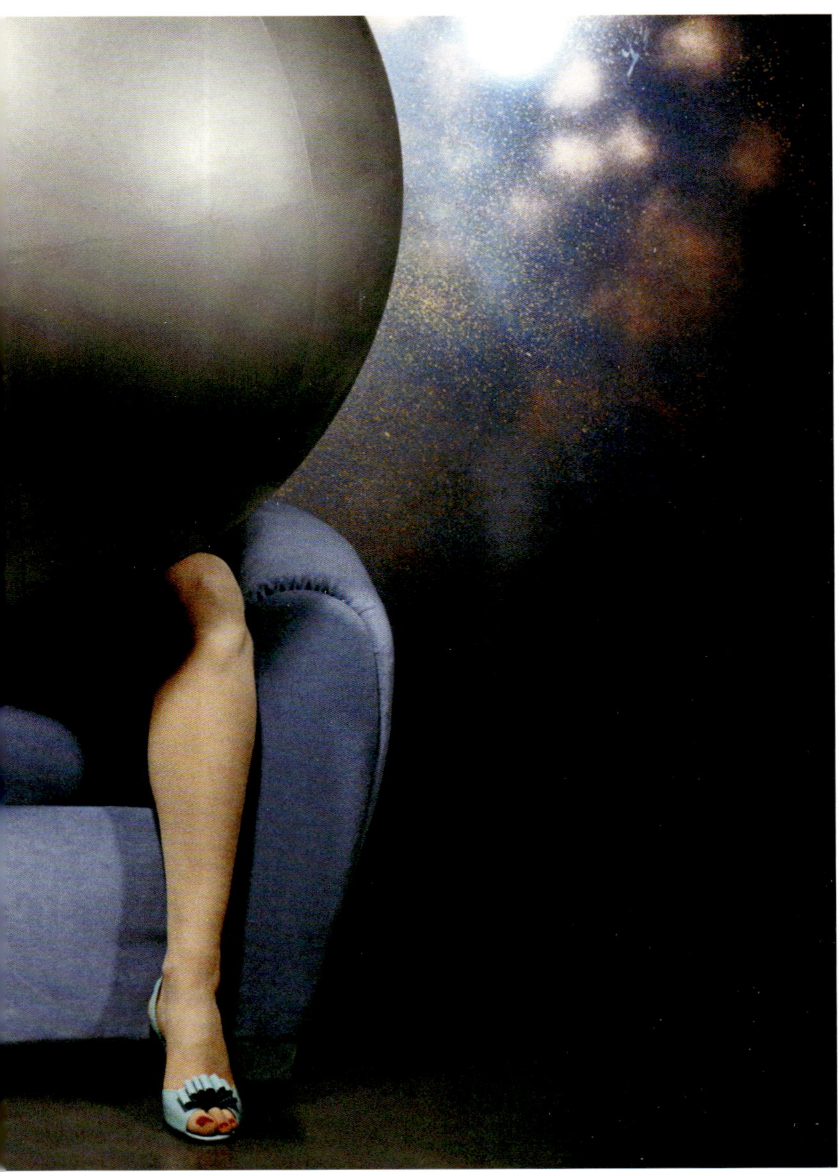

Biography

1928 Guy Louis Banarès is born on
2 December, at 7 rue Popincourt, Paris.

1929 Guy is adopted by Maurice Désiré
Bourdin, who brings him up with the help
of Marguerite Legay, his mother.

1948–49 Does military service in Dakar,
Senegal, where he receives his first
photography training as a cadet in the
French Air Force.

1950 Returns to Paris. First exhibition
of his drawings and paintings in a gallery
on the Rue de Bourgogne.

1951 Meets Man Ray and becomes his protégé.

1952 First exhibition of his photographs at
Galerie 29 in Paris. Man Ray writes the
introduction for the catalogue.

1953 Exhibition of his photographs under
the pseudonym Edwin Hallan at Galerie
Huit in Paris.

1954 Exhibition of his drawings at the
Galerie de Beaune in Paris. Meets
Edmonde Charles-Roux, editor-in-chief
of *Vogue Paris*.

1954–57 Takes part in touring photography
exhibitions organized by the C.S.
(Combined Societies) Association, UK.

1955 Publication of his first fashion shots
in the February edition of *Vogue France*.
Exhibition of his drawings at the Galerie
des Amis des Arts, Paris.
Takes part in a group exhibition called
'Chats', at the Galerie de Seine, Paris.
Exhibition of his paintings at the Galerie
Charpentier, Paris.

1956 Exhibition of his drawings at the
Galerie de Seine, Paris.

1957 Exhibition of paintings and drawings
at the Peter Deitsch Gallery, 51 East 73rd
Street, New York.
Takes part in the group exhibition 'Vogue'
at the International Photography Biennale,
Venice.

1961 Marries Solange Marie Louise Gèze.
Takes part in the exhibition 'Le Photographe
en face de son métier' at the Salon National
de la Photographie in Paris.

1964 Francine Crescent, an editor at *Vogue
Paris*, introduces him to the shoe designer
Roland Jourdan, who becomes his patron.

1965 Exhibition of his drawings at the Galerie
Jacques Desbrière, Paris.

1966 Takes part in the Photokina 66 festival
in Cologne.

1967 Birth of Samuel, his only child.
First ad campaign for Charles Jourdan
shoes. Fashion shoots for *Harper's Bazaar*
and *Photo*.

1971 Death of Solange Marie Louise Gèze.

1972 Fashion shoots for Italian *Vogue*.

1973 Ad campaign for the advertising
agency MAFIA, Paris.

1974 Fashion shoots for British *Vogue*.

1975 Ad campaign for Issey Miyake.

1976 Shoots the *Sighs and Whispers* lingerie
catalogue for Bloomingdale's, New York.
Ad campaigns include: Baila for Gianfranco
Ferré, Complice & Callaghan for Gianni
Versace, and Loewe.

1977 Fashion shoots for *Vogue Hommes*
and *20 ans*. Takes part in the exhibition
'The History of Fashion Photography',
which tours US venues including the
San Francisco Museum of Modern Art.

1978 Ad campaign for Claude Montana.
Takes part in the Photokina 78 festival
in Cologne. Calendars for Issey Miyake
and Yashica.

1980 Calendar for Pentax.

1981 Final ad campaign for Charles Jourdan.
Fashion shoots for *Linea Italiana*.

1982 Ad campaigns for Gianfranco Ferré,
Lancetti and Roland Pierre.
Takes part in the group exhibition 'Color as
Form' at George Eastman House, Rochester,
New York.

1985 Ad campaign for Emanuel Ungaro.
Turns down the Grand Prix National de
la Photographie, awarded by the French
Ministry of Culture, but his name is
retained on the list of award winners.

1986 Takes part in the Photokina 86 festival
in Cologne.

1987 End of his contract with *Vogue Paris*.
Fashion shoots for *The Best*.
Ad campaigns for Révillon and Chanel.

1988 Annie Leibovitz presents him with
the Infinity Award from the International
Center of Photography in New York.
Takes part in the Photography Triennale,
Paris.

1991 Dies in Paris on 29 March, at the age
of sixty-two.

Selected bibliography

Samuel Bourdin and Fernando Delgado,
Exhibit A: Guy Bourdin, ed. Fernando
Delgado, foreword by Luc Santé, essay
by Michel Guerrin, Boston: Blufinch Press;
and Paris: Seuil, 2001; first major monograph
on Bourdin's work

Charlotte Cotton and Shelly Verthime (eds.),
Guy Bourdin, London: V&A Publications;
New York: Harry N. Abrams, 2003

Guy Bourdin: 67 Polaroids, Paris: Star
Publishing, 2004

Alison M. Gingeras, *Guy Bourdin*, London:
Phaidon, 2006

Nicolle Meyer and Shelly Verthime,
Guy Bourdin: A Message For You,
2 vols, Göttingen: SteidlDangin, 2006

Unseen: Guy Bourdin, London: Phillips
de Pury, 2007

Guy Bourdin: Polaroids, Paris: Xavier Barral,
2009

Guy Bourdin, 'Stern Portfolio' series, no. 61,
Augsburg: teNeues, 2010

Guy Bourdin: In Between, ed. Shelly Verthime.
Göttingen: Steidl, 2010

Guy Bourdin: Britain by Cadillac, London:
Somerset House Trust, 2014

Miami: Guy Bourdin, 'Fashion Eye' series,
Paris: Louis Vuitton, 2016

Guy Bourdin: Untouched, Göttingen:
SteidlDangin, 2017

Guy Bourdin: Image Maker, texts by Matthias
Harder and Shelly Verthime, Paris: Assouline,
2017

Guy Bourdin for Charles Jourdan, ed. Patrick
Rémy, New York: Rizzoli, 2024

Selected exhibitions

Solo exhibitions

1950 Paintings and drawings, Galerie Rue
de Bourgogne, Paris.

1952 Galerie 29, Paris.

1953 Under the pseudonym Edwin Hallan,
Galerie Huit, Paris.

1981 Rencontres Internationales de la
Photographie, Arles.

1999 First posthumous exhibition:
Pace MacGill Gallery, New York.

2002 'Guy Bourdin & Anton Corbijn',
Camera Work, Berlin.

2003 'Prints for Sale from the V&A's
Guy Bourdin Show', Michael Hoppen
Gallery, London.

2003–13 'Guy Bourdin', Victoria & Albert
Museum, London; 2004: National Gallery
of Victoria, Melbourne; Jeu de Paume, Paris;
FOAM, Amsterdam; 2005: NRW Forum,
Düsseldorf; National Art Museum of China,
Beijing; 2006: Shanghai Art Museum; Tokyo
Metropolitan Museum of Photography; 2008:
Kunst Haus Wien, Vienna; FOMU, Antwerp;
2009: Moscow House of Photography,
Moscow; MuBE, São Paolo; 2011: MACRS,
Porto Alegre; 2013: Deichtorhallen, Hamburg.

2005 'Guy Bourdin', Alison Jacques Gallery,
London.

2006–22 'Guy Bourdin: A Message for You',
Peggy Guggenheim Collection, Venice;
Fondation HSBC pour la Photographie, Paris;
2007: Hollywood Centre, Hong Kong; 2008:
Today Art Museum, Beijing; 2009: Galleria
Carla Sozzani, Milan; Festival International

de la Photographie de Mode, Cannes;
2010: Sala Canal de Isabel II, Madrid; 2013:
MNAF, Florence; 2014: Louise Alexander
Gallery, Porto Cervo; 2022: Al Blu di Prussia,
Naples.

2007–10 'Guy Bourdin: Unseen', Phillips de
Pury Gallery, New York; The Wapping Project,
London; Michael Hoppen Gallery, London.

2009–10 'Guy Bourdin, ses films', Le Bon
Marché Rive Gauche, Paris; 10 Corso
Como, Seoul.

2010–17 'Guy Bourdin: In Between', French
Embassy, New York; 2017: Fondazione
Sozzani, Milan.

2012 'Guy Bourdin', Michael Hoppen
Gallery, London.

2013 'Guy Bourdin: Archives', Louise
Alexander Gallery, Porto Cervo.

2013–17 'Guy Bourdin: Untouched',
Rencontres Internationales de la
Photographie, Arles; 2017: Fondazione
Sozzani, Milan.

2014–17 'Guy Bourdin: Image Maker',
Somerset House, London; 2017:
Helmut Newton Foundation, Berlin.

2015 'Guy Bourdin. Mise en abyme',
Louise Alexander Gallery, Porto Cervo.
'Guy Bourdin: Walking Legs', Michael
Hoppen Gallery, London.

2015–17 'Guy Bourdin: Avant-garde',
Fotografiska, Stockholm; 2017:
Tbilisi Photo Festival.

2016 'Guy Bourdin: The Portraits',
Acacias Art Center, Paris.

2017 'Guy Bourdin: Feminities', Maison
Chloé, Paris.

2018 'Guy Bourdin: 50 Polaroids', Louise
Alexander Gallery, Porto Cervo.

2019 'Guy Bourdin: Zoom', Musée de la
Photographie Charles Nègre, Nice.
'Guy Bourdin: L'Image dans l'image',
Campredon Art & Image, L'Isle-sur-la-Sorgue,
France.

2020 'Guy Bourdin: Pariser Avantgarde der
Nachkriegszeit', Kunsthalle, Talstrasse, Halle.
'Follow Me', Lumière Gallery, Moscow.
'Guy Bourdin. Polaroids & photographies',
Matou, Toulouse.

2021 'The Absurd and The Sublime', Chanel
Nexus Hall, Tokyo.

2023 'Guy Bourdin: Storyteller', Armani/Silos,
Milan.

Group exhibitions

1957 First International Photography Biennale,
Venice.

1960 'Photographs for Collectors', MoMA,
New York.

1961 'Le Photographe en face de son métier',
Salon National de la Photographie, Paris.

1968 14th Milan Triennale.

1969 'L'Insolite et la Mode', Galerie Delpire,
Paris.

1977 'The History of Fashion Photography',
George Eastman House, Rochester, NY;
San Francisco Museum of Modern Art.

1982 'Color as Form', George Eastman House,
Rochester, NY.

1988 Triennale Internationale de la
Photographie, Paris.

2002 'Shine Anniversary Show', Michael
Hoppen Gallery, London.
'Archeology of Elegance', Deichtorhallen,
Hamburg.

2003 'Flesh Tones: 100 Years of the Nude',
Robert Mann Gallery, New York.
'Phantom der Lust', Neue Galerie, Graz.

2006 'The Heartbeat of Fashion',
Deichtorhallen, Hamburg.

2007 'Mode-Bilder. Fotografien aus der
Sammlung F.C. Gundlach', NRW Forum,
Düsseldorf.

2008 '*Vogue*: Les natures mortes',
Rencontres d'Arles.

2008–9 'Controverses: Une histoire éthique
et juridique de la photographie', Photo
Élysée, Lausanne; Bibliothèque Nationale
de France, Paris.

2009 'Shake It: An Instant History of The
Polaroid', Pump House Gallery, London.
'Colour', Michael Hoppen Gallery, London.

2010–12 'Exposed: Voyeurism, Surveillance &
the Camera since 1870', Tate Modern, London;
2010–12: San Francisco Museum of Modern
Art; 2011: Walker Art Center, Minneapolis.

2011 'Beauty CULTure', Annenberg Space

for Photography, Los Angeles.
'Madame Grès', Musée Bourdelle, Paris.
'Vanity', Kunsthalle, Vienna.

2012–13 'Mannequin. Le corps de la
mode', Rencontres Internationales de la
Photographie, Arles; Cité de la Mode et
du Design, Paris.
'120 Years of *Vogue* and 7 Years of *Vogue
China*', Park Hyatt Hotel, Beijing.
'Ideal Pole Part III: Style to Death',
Ramiken Crucible, New York.

2013 'Glam! The Performance of Style',
Tate, Liverpool.
'Arles in Black', Rencontres Internationales
de la Photographie, Arles.
'White: Photography, Art, Design, Fashion,
Film', Netherlands Fotomuseum, Rotterdam.

2014 'Papier glacé', Palais Galliera, Paris.

2015–16 'Coming into Fashion: A Century of
Photographs at Condé Nast', Moscow House
of Photography, Moscow.

2016 'The Image as Question', Michael
Hoppen Gallery, London.
'Elizabeth Price Curates: In a Dream You Saw
a Way to Survive and You Were Full of Joy',
Hayward Gallery, London.
'*Vogue* 100: A Century of Style', National
Portrait Gallery, London.

2017 'Like a Horse', Fotografiska, Stockholm.

2018 'Shape of Light: 100 Years of Photography
and Abstract Art', Tate Modern, London.
'Icon of Style: A Century of Fashion
Photography, 1911–2011', J. Paul Getty
Museum, Los Angeles.
'A Tribute to F.C. Gundlach: Photographer
and Collector', Christie's, Paris.
'Feast for the Eyes: The Story of Food in
Photography', FOAM, Amsterdam.

2021 '*Vogue Paris* 1920–2020', Palais Galliera,
Paris.

2024 'Apple of Discord', Louise Alexander
Gallery, Porto Cervo.

Special thanks to Samuel Bourdin for his valuable help
with this book, to Shelly Verthime and Sarah Moon,
who selected the photographs and designed the layout,
and also to Pascal Dangin for his expert eye.

The Photofile series is the original English-language edition of the Photo Poche collection. It was first published between 1986 and 1992 by the Centre National de la Photographie, Paris, with the support of the French Ministry of Culture. Robert Delpire (1926–2017) was the creator of the series and its managing editor until 2017.

General editor: Agnès Gagnès, assisted by Émeline Loric.
Series design by Matthew Young
Translated from the French

First published in the United Kingdom in 2008 by
Thames & Hudson Ltd, 181A High Holborn, London WC1V 7QX

First published in the United States of America in 2008 by
Thames & Hudson Inc., 500 Fifth Avenue, New York, New York 10110

British Library Cataloguing-in-Publication Data
A catalogue record for this book is available from the British Library
Library of Congress Catalog Card Number 2007906974

ISBN (UK): 978-0-500-41090-5
ISBN (USA): 978-0-500-41129-2

Printed and bound in Italy